Happy Birthday
Aug. 2014
Your Friends,
Gary & Mary Moce

May this book cause you
to think even more than you
have in the past and pass
your knowledge on to those
you minister to.

D1314322

the LIFE of Radical FAITH

the LIFE of Radical FAITH

JEFF KEATON

The Life of Radical Faith

Cover and Interior Design: Jennifer Wooldridge

Editor: Bill Watkins

ISBN: 978-0-9913177-0-7

jeffkeaton.net

Printed in the United States of America

First Printing, 2014

In Honor of...

The faith I possess has been graciously passed down to me from my two late grandmothers, Eleaze Cash and Nancy Keaton McKinney, and my parents, Dr. James and Carolyn Keaton. Through every wilderness in life, they never lost sight of the Promised Land.

I also want to honor every person I have ever had the privilege of leading to Christ and discipling. Their conversions to Christ and their transformed lives have forever made me a believer in the supernatural power of our life-changing Christ.

Last but not least, I want to honor the two congregations I have had the privilege of pastoring over the last two decades. These congregations in Hollywood, FL and Roanoke, VA believed in me, allowed me to sprout my faith wings, and followed my visionary leadership when at times they must have thought I was crazy.

Table of Contents

Section Three

A Desire to Serve

Section Four

A Life of Supernatural Success

Prologue

One day in 2008, as I was praying in my office, I received an impression that seemed to be from the Lord that I was to write a book entitled *Radical Faith*. I wrote this title on a piece of paper and set it aside. This impression came to me in the early days of the "New Vision" now known as Renewanation. I fully assumed that I would wait to write this book until Renewanation had grown into a fully mature ministry, about fifteen to twenty years later. However, God had different plans.

In April of 2011, I was in a meeting in Orlando, Florida with a group of men who were passionate about saving students from the onslaught of secularism by giving them a Christian worldview education. I was exhausted after preaching twice on Sunday morning and then flying to Florida for meetings all day Monday. I went to bed Monday night very discouraged—not about the response to this need but the limitations of my time and energy. How could I keep pastoring a thriving church, lead a school and summer camp, and work with our church plants while building Renewanation from the ground up? The job was humanly impossible.

After a restless night, I awoke to the solution. It was as if the clouds were gone, and God's answer for my future ministry became crystal clear. I sensed God saying, "This Fall, you will leave your church and go full-time with Renewanation. You will write two books: *Radical Faith* and *Why Christian Worldview Education in America*. And you will speak to pastors and in churches helping to spread the great mission of Christian worldview education." That was it. I knew beyond a shadow of a doubt that I had heard the voice of the Lord, even though His timing was different than mine. I had assumed this book on Radical Faith would be written later in life and that I would maintain my position as Senior Pastor for at least three more years until our youngest daughter graduated from high school. God understood that this approach would have been unsustainable for me. I was relieved.

I immediately went back to my family and congregation and shared with them what the Lord had spoken into my heart. With much excitement and joy as well as sadness of heart, I have followed the Lord's leadership into full-time service with Renewanation and into the world of writing.

While contemplating the writing of this book, I kept asking myself, "Who am I to write a book on radical faith?" I don't have a Ph.D. in faith. I don't have a Ph.D in anything. I graduated from a small Bible college and have pastored two churches for most of the last twenty years. As I will share in this book, my journey of faith has been significant in some ways, but not spectacular. So why would God ask me to write this book? The only answer that comes to mind is this: At key moments since February 11, 1990, God has asked me to live by Radical Faith, and with His grace and help I have found the strength to obey Him. As a result, I have been blessed to see Him do great things. I believe that is the story He wants me to tell, as well as give a blueprint for what a life of Radical Faith really consists of, as best I understand it.

Join me for the journey.

Chapter 1

What is Radical Faith?

Without faith it is impossible to please God.
Hebrews 11:6

Jack walked into my office deeply troubled. He and his wife were recent converts to Christ, and I knew that many good things had been happening in their lives. However, I had noticed that Jack's countenance had been troubled for a few weeks. On this day, he sat in my office with a heavy spirit and said, "Pastor, please pray for me. God is asking me to do something, but I'm scared to do it." His burden was so deep he didn't even think he could tell me, his new pastor. I encouraged Jack to obey the Lord no matter what it cost him.

A few weeks later he came bouncing into my office with his wife in tow. "Pastor," he said, "sixteen years ago, in a drunken stupor, I cheated on my wife. It was a one-night stand, but it has been haunting me since I gave my life to Christ. Over the last few weeks I have been under deep conviction. The Holy Spirit has been telling me that I must come clean with my wife if I want to become all that He wants me to be." Jack continued, "I have been so afraid. I just knew that if I told Janie, she would leave me on the spot. But, finally, I decided to obey God no matter the outcome, and I told her."

Radical Faith takes a *willingness* to sacrifice and even suffer.

As Jack talked, I observed his wife Janie. She seemed to have a sense of peace and calm about the whole situation. She had seen the transformation that Christ had brought about in her husband's life, and she was ready to forgive and move on. Over the years, I have watched this couple grow deep in the faith. They were eventually called into full-time Christian ministry. Jack went back to college, and today they are the lead pastoral family in a local church.

This is what Radical Faith looks like in action!

It took absolute surrender to God's will in order for Jack to obey Him in this situation. It took a willingness to sacrifice and even suffer. It took a deep love for God and for Janie. And it brought about supernatural success in the life of this family.

Do you want to live a life of significance? A life that truly matters on both sides of the grave? If so, it starts with a new approach to life—one built on the God who requires you to trust him completely, unreservedly. This is the life of Radical Faith. And it always produces supernatural success. All great Christians throughout history have been men and women of Radical Faith. If your heart is crying out to be a difference maker, then this is the approach to life you need to understand and fully embrace.

True and False Faith

The wonderful biblical doctrine of faith has been much maligned by individuals from very different sides of the theological spectrum. On the one hand, we find professing Christians who possess so little faith they might better be described as practicing atheists. This group lives each day as if God isn't really involved in the equation of life. They live in the flesh and rely on the flesh to live out their lives. If you ask them if they trust God, they will give you a hearty AMEN! They can even quote many of the faith passages in the Bible, but in reality they simply do not believe God enough or know Him enough to follow His lead when He wants them to move out of their comfort zone. This is the sad plight of far too many in our churches. I believe it is the main reason why so many individuals and churches are making almost no difference for God in this world.

On the other hand, we find those who have taken and twisted the doctrine of faith into a genie-in-a-bottle formula. God is treated as the great "Santa in the sky" by these precious but confused Christians. Here are a couple examples.

The day LuAnn, who was angry with God, walked into my office is forever etched into my memory. She was a remarkably talented singer at a nearby church. Her church taught that if you had enough faith, basically nothing bad could or should happen to you. Her husband was an unbeliever and was unfaithful to their marriage as well. The leaders of her church told LuAnn that if she just had enough faith, her husband could not leave her; God would not allow it. However, her husband did leave her, and she was now blaming God. "I believed with all my heart, and God failed me," she told me. With all the compassion I could muster, I answered, "God did not fail you. Your church failed you." She had been taught a view of faith that was false. It was sure to fail, and it did.

While I was in college, my wife did some babysitting for a young couple. The husband had been in a car wreck and was greatly impaired as a result. This couple decided to go to a faith healing service where a well-known televangelist was speaking. Much to their disappointment, they did not experience the healing they were hoping for. They left devastated.

Radical Faith is a deep and abiding belief in who God is, in what God says, and in what God can do, and it is a willingness to obey Him as a result of this belief.

I want to go on record that I certainly believe God still heals people in our day when He so desires. I saw a man healed from a crippling stroke when I was a child—a miracle I'll never forget. *However, the Radical Faith I am writing about is much deeper and more costly than the cold, legalistic faith that so many people think is normal, or the shallow, sensational, and often erroneous faith many others profess to have today.*

So there is no confusion, here is what I mean by Radical Faith, and it is informed by what I have learned from God's Word: *Radical Faith is a deep and abiding belief in who God is, in what God says, and in what God can do, and it is a willingness to obey Him as a result of this belief.* Of course, anyone can claim that their understanding of faith comes from Scripture. So I will spend a good deal of this book showing that what I have learned about Radical Faith is clearly anchored in God's written Word, and it has clearly shown up in God's people. I will start with the greatest summary of faith in action in Scripture—Hebrews 11.

Radical Faith in Hebrews 11

In Hebrews 11 we are given a picture of what Radical Faith really looks like in the life of an individual. Almost all of the people described in Hebrews 11 made a significant impact on the world around them and a great impression upon God Himself, as a result of their Radical Faith. However, this life of great faith was not an easy life, nor did it always lead to a happy ending here on earth. Most of these believers never saw the mature fruit of prayers answered. But no matter the cost, they continued to believe in God and obey Him.

Many of those mentioned in Hebrews 11 are well-known giants of the faith. God speaks of Abel, Enoch, Noah, Abraham, Sarah, Moses, and several others. Noah worked on his "faith project" for 120 years without a single convert outside of his family members. Abram left his homeland and headed out with only the voice of God as a guide. Moses walked away from the wealth and fame of Egypt and was asked to wait for 40 years before he became the Hebrews' instrument of deliverance from 400 years of bondage. All of these faith giants left a huge impact on the human race because they were willing to obey God.

However, there are others mentioned in Hebrews 11 whose

names we will never know in this life. These, too, knew who God was and were willing to obey Him even if it didn't work out so well here on earth. We are told that they were tempted, imprisoned, and killed with the sword. Many had to live in caves and were destitute, afflicted, and tormented.

God thought so highly of these who lived out the life of Radical Faith that He said in Hebrews 11:38, "The world was not even worthy of them."

These faith heroes all had eyes to see what those who do not trust God can never see. They knew that their obedience to the God of this universe would bring them a great reward.

Hebrews 11:6 tells us, "Without faith it is impossible to please God." Unless we believe in Him and in what He says, we will never become the people He wants us to be, and we will not do what He asks us to do. How can we please God in this way? We cannot. The life of Radical Faith takes us in a very different direction. *It is simply knowing what God wants and doing it at all times. That is Radical Faith! It is not some super spiritual, mystical, Christian state. It is far more practical and accessible than that.*

For example, years ago God specifically asked me to look to Him for career decisions, not to the pay offered. Taking Him at His word, I have never asked to know what my financial compensation would be for accepting a new ministry position. Instead, I sought God's direction first. After I received the go-ahead from Him— in other words, after I already knew He wanted me to take the position and I had agreed to take it—did I seek to learn what my compensation would be. While this is normal for me, it has certainly surprised others. I'll never forget the look on one board member's face when he asked me, "What would it take financially to get you to come to our church?" I told him I didn't want to know what they would pay me until after I had made my decision. All I needed to know was whether or not God wanted me to come to their church. The board member was stunned.

Since February 11, 1990, the only question I really need an answer to is: "What does God want me to do?" I have learned on this journey of faith that the rest will take care of itself if I am living in obedience to God's will. On paper, I probably should not have accepted any of my ministry positions; they have all had their challenges. But because I heard God's voice and obeyed His call, I have been privileged to enjoy an amazing ride with Him and some of the greatest people on earth.

Radical Faith and Obedience

A willingness to go anywhere God asks us to go and do anything He asks us to do is a sign that we are living the life of Radical Faith. I have found that for many people, this definition of Radical Faith seems too simple. We want to talk about our great faith to believe God for healing from cancer or some other disease. We want to talk about believing God to give us a huge amount of money or a new job or some other gift that will greatly enhance our ability to live a more comfortable life. However, we don't want to talk about faith as it relates to our daily obedience to Christ. What we need to grasp, though, is that we will never do anything "BIG" for God until we first learn to trust and obey Him in the "smallest" areas of life.

I have met many people who talked about their great faith, only to discover that they were living lives of willful rebellion against

God. They believed God could heal them from a physical disease, but they apparently did not believe that He has the power to help them obey His holy law.

I've known Christians who said they believed God would help them win the lotto so they could give a large gift to their church. In reality, however, they didn't trust God enough to provide for them when it came to considering whether they would give a tithe of their income each week to Him.

In contrast, Radical Faith is simply figuring out what God expects and then doing it no matter what it costs. This kind of faith is not as snazzy and stylish as what is commonly taught in our day, but it produces supernatural and eternal fruit. This kind of faith doesn't get the crowd on their feet when you're preaching about it, but it will revolutionize the life of a Christian and the life of the church, and it will drive people to their knees.

We will never do anything "BIG" for God until we first learn to trust and obey Him in the "smallest" areas of life.

I have always had a longing to make a difference with my one, simple life. I have studied the lives of men and women across history, especially those who have made the greatest difference for Christ. I have concluded that all of them had discovered the secret of living a life of Radical Faith. Against all odds, they were willing to obey God because they believed He knew best. They were also people who knew God well enough to know what He expected of them individually and personally.

David Brainerd, a great young missionary who died in his

efforts to take the gospel to the American Indians, was a man who made a huge difference for God because of his radical trust in God. He said, "Lord let me make a difference for You that is utterly disproportionate to who I am." That is my prayer as well. And I realize that the only way to do this is to understand what God expects from me and trust Him by being 100 percent obedient to His plan.

In the pages ahead, we will look at what the life of Radical Faith consists of, and I will do my best to give you biblical and contemporary examples of this most rewarding life. I will tell you what I have learned and experienced about this life. In short, what I will show you is that the life of Radical Faith is a life of ...

- Absolute surrender to God's will and way

- A willingness to suffer and sacrifice in order to obey God

- Passionate service to God and man

- Supernatural success

Section I

A Life of Absolute Surrender to God

Chapter 2

Does God Expect A Fully Surrendered Life?

The Problem

It seems like in almost every church there are two classes of Christians: the sold out, totally surrendered believers, and the half-hearted, non-surrendered believers. It usually falls along the 20/80 percentage lines known as the Pareto principle. Twenty percent are sold out and totally committed. They give 80 percent of the finances necessary to operate the ministry and do 80 percent of the work. The other 80 percent of believers attend church, occasionally pay their tithe, and hold on to their ticket to heaven. It doesn't matter what church you attend or which theological group you're a part of, this principle generally holds true.

Local churches have grown so accustomed to this dichotomy that it hardly seems to alarm us anymore. However, is this really what God expects or desires from Christians? Not hardly.

The Solution

In Mark 12:28-31, Jesus was asked the question. "Which is the first commandment of all?" Jesus replied, "And you shall love the Lord your God with all your heart, with all your soul, with all your mind and with all your strength. This is the first commandment." Without trying to dissect exactly what Jesus meant by heart, soul, mind, and strength, we can all agree that the greatest commandment ever given is a command that calls us to be 100 percent committed and surrendered to Christ. This is what God expects from every Christian. This commandment was not just given to a few white-haired saints or expected of just the likes of a Mother Theresa or a Billy Graham. This commandment, to surrender all to God, was given to every individual who desires to have Christ as his or her Lord and Savior.

The greatest commandment calls us to be 100 percent *committed* and *surrendered* to Christ.

It is amazing to what lengths we will go to avoid obeying this first and greatest commandment. We will conform to a list of outward rules. We will change our behavior. We will get involved in helping others and working in a church. We will do all kinds of things if it will help us avoid coming to the place of *total surrender* to God's will for our lives. We are all born with an inner resistance towards surrendering to authority, especially God's authority. It scares most of us half to death to think about turning the controls of our lives completely over to God. I well remember this unfounded fear I possessed as a teenager. I was afraid of what God might ask me to do if I surrendered my all to Him. Satan made me think that God's plan was somehow inferior to my plan. Oh how I wish I had trusted the Lord more in those days.

In Luke 18:18-23, a rich young ruler approaches Jesus. He asks the all-important question, "Good Teacher, what shall I do to inherit eternal life?" Jesus gives him a list of the five horizontal commandments—the section of the Ten Commandments that deals with how we are to treat each other and what we own. The young ruler quickly responds: "All these I have kept from my youth." And then Jesus gets to the core issue of absolute surrender to God: "You still lack one thing. Sell all that you have and distribute to the poor, and you will have treasure in heaven; and come, follow Me." When the rich young ruler heard that he would have to surrender his dearest possessions, he walked away very sad because he wasn't willing to pay the price Jesus required. He was a very good and moral man. Jesus did not refute his claim that he had obeyed all the commandments that most of us broke in our youth. He would have been the perfect church board member. He was the kind of guy you would have wanted handling your money. And yet, Jesus told him that in order to receive the gift of eternal life, he would have to surrender fully to God in every area of his life and make God his first and highest focus and commitment.

Had this young ruler fully surrendered to God, we would likely know his name today. He would have gone on to do great things for God. However, because he was unwilling to fully surrender, he probably never fulfilled the plan God had for his life.

Maybe you're reading this book, and you know you haven't reached your full potential in Christ and consequently in life yet. Let me ask you, have you fully surrendered every part of your being to Christ? We cannot live the life of Radical Faith until we trust God enough to fully yield every part of our life to Him.

The Amazing Potential

I believe the key to a great spiritual awakening, personally and corporately in America and in other parts of the world, is as simple as believers getting off the fence and fully surrendering to all that God has for them. I've seen personal revival break out in my own life as well as in the lives of others when surrendering all to Christ occurs. We all know those who are sold out. Go to any church and ask the simple question, "Who here is completely sold out to Jesus?" Within moments names will roll off people's lips. I know that we cannot judge the heart of a man or a woman, but the person who is 100 percent surrendered to Christ cannot hide their love and passion for Him. The Christ life is evident for all to see.

What if every pastor was fully surrendered to Christ? What if every Sunday school teacher was too? What if every Christian no matter their role or occupation was 100 percent surrendered to God's will and way? What kind of impact would we have on this sin-cursed and darkened world? The greatest hindrance to the spreading of the gospel is Christians who are not fully yielded to the Lordship of Christ. Half-hearted Jesus followers end up living hypocritical lives before their fellow man and become a source of immunization against the acceptance of Christ. I have heard many people say, "If that is what a Christian is, then I surely don't want to be one." However, the fragrance and power of a fully surrendered life is overwhelming and powerful to the searching heart.

After one occasion when I preached on this subject, I walked past the front receptionist desk the following week and saw a precious seventy-four-year-old lady named Micky answering phones. She was one of our many volunteers who would attend to the phones as well as volunteer in our Christian school. On numerous occasions I would see her walking the halls or sitting down with a student who needed tutoring. Often the child she was with would be one of our more rambunctious students who struggled to pay close attention. It didn't matter to Micky. She had the patience of Job and the love of Jesus. Everywhere I turned she was volunteering in the church or school. Even in her mid-seventies, she was working more diligently for Christ than most thirty-year olds. She was also heavily involved with children through another inner-city ministry. It wasn't uncommon for her to pick up a child from the projects and take him or her to purchase school clothes or supplies. She is one sold-out lady for Christ.

> The fragrance and power of a *fully* surrendered life is overwhelming and powerful to the searching heart.

As I walked past her that morning, she said, "Pastor Jeff, you know that sermon you preached on Sunday about being 100 percent sold out to Jesus?"

"Yes," I said.

She continued, "I just hope that someday I will be one of those completely sold-out Christians."

I looked at Micky and said, "You are one of those sold-out Christians, and if I could find a bunch more just like you, we could change the world."

Here's what I've found. Those who are most fully surrendered to Christ don't always know it and surely don't talk about it much. However, many who are not, seem to think they are and will make sure you know it.

Surrendered **people are beautiful people.**

In Micky's younger days, she was a transcriptionist for U.S. Presidents Johnson, Nixon, and Ford. She traveled the world with them and typed everything they said in meetings. Now, because of her full devotion to Christ and the people He loves, she sits on a couch with a child who has attention deficit disorder and teaches the child how to read. Surrendered people are beautiful people, and they give of themselves fully and humbly.

The Way Forward

In Romans 12:1, the Apostle Paul gives us this great challenge: "Therefore, I urge you, brothers, in view of God's mercy, to offer your bodies as living sacrifices, holy and pleasing to God—this is your spiritual act of worship" (NIV). I think most of us would agree that Paul here was addressing men and women who had already made their initial surrender to Christ at conversion. He calls them brothers. He used this title often when talking to fellow Christians. But here in Romans 12:1 Paul urges these Christians to go to a newer and deeper level of surrender now that they were alive in

Christ and had a deeper understanding of what it meant to follow Him completely. Paul's initial readers knew what it meant to offer a body as a sacrifice. After all, they had seen animals sacrificed in the various Roman temples, and they knew that once an animal had been chosen for this ritual, it had no more say over its future. Of course, Paul is not urging his readers to think of themselves as animals in God's hands. He calls on them to give themselves to God freely, humbly, and reverently. He wants them to use their freedom in Christ to commit themselves unreservedly to Him. He has already given Himself to them, even sacrificing His life for them. Now it is time for them to respond to Him as He has to them.

Jesus prayed, "Not My will but Yours be done," and He walked straight to the cross.

What was true for them is true for us. If we are going to find the strength and courage to live a life of Radical Faith, it will happen because we have offered our lives as living sacrifices to God. We have laid down our spirit of resistance, and we have nothing but a great big "Yes, God" in our hearts. There's a little chorus that simply says, "My heart says yes, yes, yes; my heart says yes, yes, yes. My heart says yes, Lord, my heart says yes, Lord. My heart says yes, yes, yes." This repetitive but sweet little chorus states where we must live if we want to make a great difference for Christ in this world.

As a part of being fully man, Jesus had to face the dilemma of complete surrender to the heavenly Father's will. In the Garden of Gethsemane, Jesus looked at what obedience to the Father was going to cost Him. In His humanity he was driven to ask if there was another way to save lost mankind. But, quickly He prayed, "Not My will but Yours be done," and He walked straight to the cross. His faith in the Father's plan and His willingness to follow that plan produced the possibility that you and I can be saved from sin and its awful consequences.

When we believe God enough to obey Him at all cost, amazing things come to pass in our lives and ministries. God longs to use people for His honor and glory if only we will fully surrender to His plan for our lives.

Chapter 3

Surrender in Scripture

If a doctrine is truly biblically based, it will be seen clearly in the Scriptures, and Christians from a great variety of backgrounds will experience it universally. I grew up in the deeper life movement, and we had a unique way of expressing our need for the infilling of the Holy Spirit. I have read from men and women who refuted our terminology but in practical experience testified to what I understand as the deeper life experience. We Christians may differ on how we understand or explain something, but if we are talking about something that is true, genuinely biblical, we will find Christians across our various faith traditions experiencing that truth.

As we think about the fact that the life of Radical Faith is a life of complete surrender to God, we need to first see if this is what God required of men and women in the Bible. Let's take a look at several well-known biblical characters, beginning with the first human pair.

Adam and Eve

When God created Adam and Eve and placed them in paradise, sin was not a part of the human experience. God gave them dominion over the world and everything was very good (Gen. 1:31). However, even in this setting, God still expected Adam and Eve to live fully surrendered lives to His plan. What was His plan? He instructed them that they could eat of all the trees in the garden except one (Genesis 1:27-31; 2:8, 15-25). Even without sin in their nature, Adam and Eve still had the potential to wrest control of their lives from God.

Along comes Satan. He begins a process of confusing Eve over what God had said and what He really expected. Satan ends up lying to Eve and convincing her that God did not have her best interest at heart. So she chose to defy God's command, and Adam followed her sin (3:1-7). The rest is tragic history.

One of the things I have noticed across the years is: When we are struggling to fully surrender to God, it is always because we do not believe He has our best interest at heart, or we do not believe that He has the ability to meet our needs. Satan uses these lies all the time. God says, "Do not lie." Satan says, "If you tell the truth in this situation, you may lose your job." So, we think about it: "Should I tell the truth? Everyone else fudges on this issue." Or Satan says, "If your spouse finds out what you did, she will be upset."

So we debate whether or not we should tell our spouse the truth about our actions.

There's a much better way to live, and it begins with our submission to God. You see, *when we are living the fully surrendered life, we refuse to disobey God, even if it means we might lose our job or our spouse may be unhappy with us.* We trust God enough to know that if we do what is right, He will take care of us. Or, like Job, even if He decides to allow us to suffer, we continue to believe that He knows best and is worthy of our trust and obedience.

One area where many people struggle to live a life of Radical Faith is in the area of relationships, specifically when looking for a husband or wife. The pull of the flesh is so powerful, and infatuation is so intoxicating that we seem to resist God's voice in this most crucial decision of life. This also tragically happens with the allure of an extramarital affair.

When we trust God supremely and are willing to wait until we know for sure He is supporting something, we save ourselves a world of heartache. My greatest regrets in life have been a result of resisting the Holy Spirit's leadership and consequently failing to trust Him enough to stay fully surrendered to His will. *I have learned that living the life of full surrender to God is the greatest safeguard against making a major mistake in life.* As long as God is in full control, we will not mess up our lives. Someone else might bring great trouble to us, but it

Living the life of full *surrender* to God is the greatest safeguard against making a major mistake in life.

will not be a result of our actions, and we will find divine grace to make it through.

Adam and Eve could have resisted Satan's temptations and obeyed God. If they had, how much different human history would have been.

Let's consider another biblical example—the first human king of the Hebrews in Israel.

King Saul

Saul started out on fire for God. He had the call of God, the anointing of God, and the priest Samuel's blessing (1 Samuel 10:1-9). He looked good on the outside, and all the people loved him. How could this guy possibly go wrong? Success had been handed to him on a silver platter. However, Saul had a problem—an obedience problem. He was impatient, and he did not trust God's way or timing.

We first see his failure to fully surrender to God in 1 Samuel 13. Saul was waiting on Samuel to come and offer a sacrifice before leading his army into battle against the Philistines. The men of Saul's army were in a panic, so Saul took charge. Rather than obey the Lord and wait for Samuel, he rationalized that it would be acceptable—even prudent—for him to offer the burnt and peace offerings—sacrifices Samuel was supposed to make. As soon as he offered the sacrifices, Samuel showed up.

> And Samuel said, "What have you done?" Saul said,
> "When I saw that the people were scattered from me,
> and that you did not come within the days appointed,

and that the Philistines gathered together at Micmash, then I said, 'The Philistines will now come down on me at Gilgal, and I have not made supplication to the Lord.' Therefore I felt compelled, and offered a burnt offering." And Samuel said to Saul, "You have done foolishly. You have not kept the commandment of the Lord your God, which He commanded you. For now the Lord would have established your kingdom over Israel forever. But now your kingdom shall not continue. The Lord has sought for Himself a man after His own heart, and the Lord has commanded him to be commander over His people because you have not kept what the Lord commanded you" (1 Samuel 13:11-14).

Saul's refusal to surrender to the Lord did not stop with this incident. Later he refused to follow the Lord's instructions to destroy the Amalekites. Again, he rationalized his sin and even spiritualized it by saying that he was not responsible, that the people had spared the best animals to sacrifice to the Lord (1 Samuel 15:1-21). Listen to his exchange with the priest Samuel after this incident.

So Samuel said, "When you were little in your own eyes, were you not head of the tribes of Israel? And did not the Lord anoint you king over Israel? Now the Lord sent you on a mission and said, 'Go, and utterly destroy the sinners, the Amalekites, and fight against them until they are consumed.' Why then did you not obey the voice of the Lord? Why did you swoop down on the spoil, and do evil in the sight of the Lord?" And Saul said to Samuel, "But I have obeyed the voice of the Lord, and gone on the mission which the Lord sent me, and brought back Agag king of Amalek. I have utterly destroyed the Amalekites. But the *people* took of the plunder, sheep and oxen, the best of the things that which should have been utterly destroyed, to sacrifice to the Lord your God in Gilgal." So Samuel said, "Has the Lord as great delight in burnt offerings and sacrifices, as in obeying the voice of the Lord? Behold to obey is better than sacrifice, and to heed than the fat of rams. For rebellion is as the sin of witchcraft, and stubbornness is as iniquity and idolatry. Because you have rejected the word of the Lord, He has also rejected you from being king" (1 Samuel 15:17-23, emphasis mine).

What a tragic picture of the cost of failing to live a life of full surrender to God. *Saul wasted his life, all because he thought he knew better than God.* Saul actually got to the place where he convinced himself that he was obeying the Lord through his acts of disobedience.

This is the sad story of every believer who refuses at any point to continuously live the surrendered life. I have discovered that before a person will do wrong, he must first of all convince himself that he is doing right. First John 1:7 stresses the importance of walking in the light of truth God gives us. If we fail to do so, we end up walking in darkness. There right looks wrong and wrong looks right; nothing seems as it is.

The church is littered today with the carcasses of those who once had high hopes of doing something significant for God in this world. But because of their refusal to fully surrender to God, they never learned to live the life of Radical Faith. Consequently, today they are just a shell of what they could have been.

Each of us can have so much better. Every believer who continuously says yes to God will walk into an ever-deepening relationship and fellowship with God. This is what simple surrender can do.

Saul wasted his life, all because he thought he knew better than God.

Enough of the negative examples. Let's look at some who learned the joy of full surrender and consequently lived the life of Radical Faith. We'll begin with a man God used to start life anew.

Noah

Thus Noah did; according to all that God commanded him, so he did.
Genesis 6:22

I have great admiration for Noah's Radical Faith. His willingness to surrender to God's divine plan—a plan that would certainly bring Noah a great deal of ridicule from his neighbors—is simply amazing. First of all, he was the only man on earth in his day who still had faith in God. We think it's difficult to be faithful to God in a world with millions of devoted Christians, Christian music, books, role models, and all the rest. How difficult must it have been in a world where sin had completely overrun humanity. Noah did not have a Bible, a church as we understand church, or any other source of support. And yet, he knew God enough to hear His voice, and he trusted God enough to do what he was asked to do. Noah surely had a thousand questions about how all this ark and flood stuff was going to work out, but for 120 years he remained fully surrendered to God's plan. That is incredible!

In our success-driven culture, Noah was an obvious failure.

So Noah's long, tedious, and arduous work building a huge ship must have brought him outstanding success in his service for God. People must have heard about his faith and been attracted to the God he worshipped. Right? Wrong. While Noah decade after decade lived in a state of full surrender to God and His plan, he never had a single convert outside of his own family. Not one person believed what Noah was preaching. His daily submission to God brought no outside tangible results. In our success-driven culture, he was an obvious failure.

Still, he obeyed. He did what God told him to do. In the process, he was laying the foundation for the salvation of humanity though only his family believed him.

Noah is a fine example of what it may mean when we surrender our lives to God. On the outside, we may look like failures. Our results may not measure up to expected standards. No matter. The results are God's. The obedience is ours.

This kind of surrender to God's will is greatly needed in our world today. The average pastor stays three to five years in a church. The average youth pastor stays a much shorter period of time. Small group leaders or Sunday school teachers invest a year or two and then bail out. Christians hop from church to church never really putting down the kind of roots necessary to build a lasting and significant ministry. We give up on our co-workers and neighbors after inviting them to church a time or two. We expect the quick fix, rapid results. We count on success—not as God understands it but as our society expects it. So when the success we want does not come, or it does not come as easily as we had hoped, we tend to search for someplace else to plant ourselves, and we even convince ourselves that this is what God wants for us too. In reality, we are living uncommitted and unsurrendered lives.

Why do we give up so quickly? Why do we expect results that may not be coming? I think this occurs for one of two reasons: Either we are not close enough to God to know what He expects from us, or we are simply unwilling to obey Him when He speaks. If we are going to experience and enjoy the life of Radical Faith, we must know God intimately so we can clearly discern what He wants us to do. Once we know what He desires from us, it's a simple matter of trust and obedience. Everything else is in His domain, under His control.

So how did all of this work out for Noah? He, his wife, and his family were saved from the worldwide judgment on humankind. Through them, God restarted the human race.

We'll talk more about Noah later on, but let's move to another man who fully surrendered to God's plan and lived the life of Radical Faith.

Abraham

"I will make you a great nation, I will bless you and I will make your name great and you shall be a blessing."
Genesis 12:2

In Genesis 12, God swoops down out of seemingly nowhere and gives Abram this call to leave the land he knew and follow Him into the unknown. With this commission comes a great promise from God: "I will make you a great nation, I will bless you and I will make your name great and you shall be a blessing" (Gen. 12:2). As we look at Abraham and beyond, keep this in mind: Even though God's success and blessing often look much different than what the world calls success, God greatly blesses those who fully surrender to His will. We'll talk a lot more about this in the last section of this book. Now, back to Abram (also called Abraham). Abram, like Noah, wasn't living in a world with millions upon millions of God-followers around. He no doubt knew about his ancestor Noah and the worldwide flood, but he was far removed from this great move of God. *However, when God made Himself clear to Abram, he surrendered fully to God's radical plan, and as a result, he fulfilled his unique and supernatural role in the history of the world.*

All of Abram's usefulness to God depended upon his willingness to surrender to God's call upon his life. We like to look back at men and women in the Bible and think, well it was easier for them; after all, they were Bible characters. Really? When God called Abram to abandon the familiar—to leave his comfort zone—he wasn't a Bible character. He was a common person just like we are. It was just as hard for him to pack up and leave as it would be for us. In fact, it was probably more difficult for Abram. He didn't have the benefit of modern communication or speed and safety of travel. His move meant that he would never again speak to or see most of his family members, friends, and work associates.

The *success* of our life depends upon our level of surrender and obedience to God's call.

God has a different plan for every person He creates. Some are called to do great things that many know about. Most are called to do great things that only God and a handful of people will ever know about. No matter what we are called to do in this life, the success of our life depends upon our level of surrender and obedience to God's call.

Had Abram said to God, "I will not leave my country," we would never have known his name. However, because of his surrender and obedience, he is listed in God's faith hall of fame (Heb. 11:8-19).

Most Christians today never do anything of great significance for God because they are unwilling to follow His plan. What would God do with your life if you fully surrendered it to Him?

There are numerous biblical examples that help us understand God's call to a life of total surrender and Radical Faith, but let me just mention a couple more.

Moses

As we continue to examine these men from the Bible, one thing continuously stands out to me. *In every case, God made His plan and will clearly known.* Noah, Abraham, and now Moses had no doubts about what God expected of them. This is a principle that has directed me for years now. I've often told my parishioners, "God wants you to know His will more than you want to know it." This is a comforting thought to me. I've heard many people say, "I just don't know what God wants me to do in life." When I hear this response, several things come to my mind. First, the Bible makes it very clear what God expects from all of us, at least in a general sense. We are all called to repent and trust Christ for the forgiveness of our sins. That is the starting point. After this we are all called to walk in all the truth or light God gives us. As we do this, He unveils His plan to us one day and situation at a time. Often, those who are struggling to find His will have missed one or both of these basic steps. We cannot know God's plan or specific will for our lives until we sincerely have a relationship with God and are living a life of full obedience, as best we understand. Disobedience, even in seemingly small areas, will prevent us from understanding God's will in other areas, especially the "big ones."

God wants you to *know* His will more than you want to know it.

As we walk with the Lord and learn to discern His voice, we still face times of uncertainty and confusion. However, as we wait patiently and walk in the Spirit and not in the flesh, He makes His plans known to us. My advice has always been, "If you do not have a sense that this is right and have a sense of peace about it, wait until you do. If you have to push, pull, and shove to make it happen, slow down." God's will is often accompanied by lots of hard work, but if God is in something, you will know it, and He will confirm it through many different means.

Moving to South Florida to take my first church was a life-changing experience. I grew up much of my young life in rural Indiana. There I was sheltered from much of the evil in the world. This all changed when I went to south Florida. My family and I moved into our tiny house near a very busy street. There were X-rated bookstores nearby, and it wasn't uncommon for someone addicted to drugs, alcohol, or sex to wander in front of our house. At times I literally felt like God had dropped us just north of hell.

I was driving down 441 getting ready to turn left onto Hollywood Boulevard one day. I was seriously troubled about this new world God had called me to live in. I asked the Lord, "Why am I here? Just to learn how to preach to this little congregation? How long do I have to stay here? When can I move back up north to a much safer place?" Suddenly, the Lord spoke boldly into my heart and mind: "Jeff, I want you to act as if you're going to be here the rest of your life, and if I ever choose to move you, I'll make it so clear you can't miss it." A deep peace came over me from that day until the day the Lord made my departure so clear I couldn't miss it. That was seven and a half years later.

I don't know when it was, but at some point in Moses' young life, he discovered that he belonged to the Hebrews. He was no doubt enjoying the benefits of being the grandson of Pharaoh. We know that he was schooled in all the wisdom of the Egyptians (Acts 7:20-22). He enjoyed all the trappings of extravagant wealth, fame, and honor. In the midst of living the high life, God began to speak to him and call him to a completely different life. I don't know what the experiences were, but I am confident that there were a few defining moments when Moses had to decide whether or not he would surrender fully to God's plan for his life. I'm sure he had no idea what all it would involve, but he had to know that it would be nothing like what he had grown up with.

We know he made a conscious choice, at some point, to identify with the Hebrews because of what we read in Hebrews 11:24-25: "By faith, Moses, when he became of age, refused to be called the son of Pharaoh's daughter, choosing rather to suffer affliction with the people of God than to enjoy the passing pleasures of sin." God asked Moses to surrender everything he had received at the hands of the Egyptians. Moses obeyed, and he subsequently changed the world forever. This had to be an unbelievably difficult decision. He walked away from everything this world calls success. His family members in Pharaoh's house must have thought he had lost his mind. His childhood and lifelong Egyptian friends must have been baffled. Surely someone tried to talk him out of choosing to identify with the people of his birth, but he chose to stay the course God had for him.

How far are you and I willing to go in order to fully yield our lives and futures to Christ? Are we willing to go as far as Moses did? How would God use your life if you surrendered everything to Him?

The Apostle Paul

The apostle Paul's story never ceases to amaze me. Sometimes God decides to rattle the world of an unbeliever in order to make His point. Paul was a Jew zealous for his heritage and utterly opposed to those believers who followed Jesus as their Messiah. In Acts 9, we find Paul traveling from city to city persecuting these Christ followers. He is absolutely convinced he is on the side of truth and righteousness as he strives to capture and lead these believers to Jerusalem for trial and execution. He has already overseen the stoning of the Christian deacon Stephen (Acts 6:5, 8-14; 7:54-8:1). But while Paul is traveling to Damascus, God suddenly and literally stops him in his tracks, and Paul becomes what he had hunted—a Christ follower (9:1-22).

One might say, "Sure Paul surrendered, but he had no choice. Anyone presented with these circumstances would surrender to God." Are you sure? How about Pharaoh? He saw the power of God over and over again but refused to yield to the one true God (Exodus 5-14).

When Christ appeared to Paul, this misguided Jew asked the all-important question as he was lying on the ground blinded by the heavenly Light: "Lord, what do you want me to do?" Jesus immediately said, "Arise and go into the city, and you will be told what you must do" (Acts 9:6). And this he did, with some help from his traveling companions. From Paul's first experience with Jesus on the road to Damascus until his final moments before his execution under the Roman emperor Nero, he lived a life of full surrender and Radical Faith. Once he knew what God expected, it was a settled matter for him. As a result, he wrote most of the New Testament books, evangelized and planted churches

> **Once Paul knew what God expected, it was a *settled* matter for him.**

throughout the Mediterranean world, and inspired Christians and even many non-Christians down through the centuries. He changed the world for Christ.

I love to read Paul's valedictory in 2 Timothy 4:6-8: "For I am already being poured out as a drink offering, and the time of my departure is at hand. I have fought the good fight, I have finished the race, I have kept the faith." These are the words of a man who sold out to Jesus for a lifetime, living the life of Radical Faith.

Making It Personal

As of this writing, I now find myself at the mid-point of life. For most of the last twenty years I have been blessed to lead two thriving churches as well as plant churches and start several other ministries. I think I have lived the life of Radical Faith to some small degree. However, at a time when a lot of us start coasting and resting on past victories, God has asked me to risk everything to follow Him to a brand new level of Radical Faith. As I have obeyed Him, there has come into my life a strange peace in the midst of serious uncertainty. Is this new life easy? Not at all. Do I hope that I will soon see more financial stability in our new ministry and in my personal life? Of course. And yet, I can honestly say that I am grateful to God for calling me to this new level of faith. I sincerely want to live by faith—serious, radical faith until the day I die. For I know and am convinced that the life of Radical Faith is the only life that produces long-term, spiritual fruit. I'm not different than you or anyone else. It is just that I have learned that in order to do anything eternal and supernatural, we must hear God's voice and obey, no matter the cost.

As you read about these great men of the Bible you might have thought, "Is that really what God expects of me?" I believe so. Billions of people stand at the edge of eternity today. Most of them will die and face certain punishment for their sin. We serve a God, though, who has gone on record as telling us that His desire is that no one should perish (2 Peter 3:9). So why do so many die without Christ? Because there are not enough men and women fully surrendered to God in this world to reach out to them in time. *If all of us lived at the same level of commitment and surrender that the apostle Paul did, we too could change the world and be Christ's life preservers to untold numbers of people.*

If you are not living the surrendered life, what is holding you back? Do you really believe your way is better?

Chapter 4

The Life of Full Surrender

There are amazing stories of great people who are living lives of Radical Faith in the 21st century. Some of the greatest stories are well known and documented in Christian circles today—stories like Jim and Carol Cymbala and the Brooklyn Tabernacle church/choir, Bob Coy at Calvary Chapel in Ft. Lauderdale, the late Jerry Falwell, and many, many others. However, in this book, I have chosen mostly to tell stories of people with whom I have had personal contact, including my own story. I do not for a moment think that I have reached a great level of Radical Faith, but I am on the journey and will share part of my story.

I first began to learn about the life of Radical Faith while watching my parents live it out every day. They came from somewhat broken and extremely humble backgrounds. Just a few days before my father was born, his father was killed in WWII. His mother, who now had five children, soon married a man to help her raise them. Though I want to honor my step-grandfather, he was not a godly influence on my father in many ways. However, my grandmother was a faithful servant of God.

Nancy Keaton McKinney

One of my great privileges in life was having Grandma McKinney around long enough for me to get to know her. When I was a kid I simply saw her as a grandma who cut my hair quite short and wasn't afraid to spank me if I misbehaved. She also knew how to cook up some great apples for breakfast. It wasn't until I grew into adulthood, married, and began visiting her with my wife that I really began to hear Grandma's story. On these visits, with no one else around, she told me about her journey of faith. I want to share it with you as best I remember those conversations.

Grandma was born and raised in the mountains of West Virginia. Her family was godless when she was a child. And yet, when she was about nine years old, she developed a great desire to know if there was a God. One day her entire family was out working in the fields, and she was left in the house to prepare meals. Home alone, she began to reach out to God. She prayed, "God, I want to know if you really exist." She asked God if she could see Him so she would know He was real. Suddenly, a voice spoke to her and said, "You cannot see my face or you will die." She ended up sitting on a porch swing that had a direct view of a mountain. As she was sitting there crying out to a God she didn't know existed, she saw what she described as flowing garments sweeping over the top of the mountain. She was suddenly overwhelmed with the knowledge that God was real. From that moment on she never again doubted His existence.

For a number of years she did not own a Bible, but she said that God continued to speak to her. One day as she was communing with God, He spoke and said, "This is my Son, Jesus, now follow Him." When she finally got her hands on a Bible, she told me that many of the Scriptures she read she already knew because of her communion with God through the years. God had supernaturally rescued my grandmother from utter darkness.

Throughout my dad's childhood, my grandmother remained faithful to God. She lived a very difficult life as her husband moved her constantly and was often unfaithful to her in many ways. My dad told me that she would often take him out on the porch of their latest shanty, pick up her guitar, and teach him about the love of Jesus. My dad attended all kinds of different churches as a child because everywhere they moved Grandma would find the closest church and lead her children to it. She loved and obeyed Jesus in the midst of her painful life.

She told us about one occasion when her husband was out all night being unfaithful. Her heart was heavy and broken, and she reached out to God to help her. As she was lying alone on her bed, a bird landed on her windowsill in the middle of that dark night and began singing. She had never heard that type of bird sing at night, but it sang until the sun rose and then flew off. She had no doubt that this bird's nightlong concert was a gift from her loving heavenly Father.

My grandmother's willingness to stay faithful and obedient to God, even when her life was hard, produced five children who all came to know Christ. Four of them have even served in Christian ministry. And many of her grandchildren and great grandchildren are now serving Christ.

We need a revival of men and women like Grandma Keaton McKinney. She lived a life of Radical Faith, and it has produced supernatural results. She never got rich. As a matter of fact, my dad bought her land and her old trailer before she died, so she wouldn't lose them. Her kids paid for her funeral because she left this world materially poor. Her husband never became a knight in shining armor for her, but she loved him tenderly until the day he died. However, her faith in God and her willingness to remain obedient to Him produced unbelievable spiritual fruit. She never got to see half of the fruit her life has produced, but someday she will know, if she doesn't already know in heaven.

Great Expectations and God-Honoring Trust

My grandmother's faithfulness and sacrifice flies in the face of our instant gratification society. Today too many of us try God out, and if He changes our lives for the better within a short period of time, we'll stick with Him, but always expecting Him to deliver quickly. If He falls short of our expectations, we try the next quick fix. For example, we may pray for our spouse, and as long as we see results, we'll stay in the marriage. If that doesn't happen, we may find some excuse to break our vow to God and our spouse and find satisfaction in another. We'll offer up our tithe as long as God gives us a good job and we aren't struggling. But as soon as the economy drops, we abandon obedience and start living in the flesh. We want results—now! We want happiness—now! And we want both without struggle, without sacrifice, without any real challenges to our faith. Such occurrences are clear signs of an American church filled with shallow, spiritual infants. Mature believers are hard to find; they are certainly not the norm, though they should be.

I remember a very nice man who was attending my church. He was conscientious about correct theology and conservative in his political views. He was a "by the book" kind of guy. One day someone said to me, "Did you know that 'so and so' has a job selling a product that is sinful and destructive?" I was surprised. This man surely would have taken a stand against using this product on a personal level. As a matter of fact, I am certain he would have thought it was a sin to use this product. However, because he needed the money that selling this product provided, he was willing to compromise his principles. I love this brother to this day, but the life of Radical Faith is a life that obeys God no matter the cost. It is a life that says, "I will do what is right even if I starve to death."

The Devil loves to tell us that we will not survive, or we will go bankrupt if we obey God. He doesn't want us to trust the One who is absolutely trustworthy. God, however, proves Himself over and over again. Because God loves His own, especially those who trust and obey Him, He enjoys blessing them and taking care of them. His blessing and care may not come to us in the ways we expect or according to our timetable. But it has been my experience and that of countless others that God meets the needs of His spiritual sons and daughters in ways they see and know, ways that humble and exalt, ways that exhibit abundant grace and love. I have seen this repeatedly in my own life as well as in the lives of others.

One of my first jobs was at a Pizza Hut delivery store in Indianapolis, Indiana. Because of my upbringing, I had a strong work ethic and tended to work circles around my fellow employees. It didn't take long for management to notice. They offered me a management position with much better pay, so I agreed to take it. Then my manager told me, "There's just one thing you will have to change. You will now have to work on Sundays." When I initially interviewed for the job, I told them that I went to church on Sundays, so I wouldn't be available to work then. Now I was being told that this commitment of mine was unacceptable for the new position. I thought about this for a moment and quickly decided that I didn't want the extra money if it meant I had to work on Sundays. I turned down the position. A short time later, God gave me another job where I made considerably more money and had a lot more potential for growth and development. God honored my faith commitment to Him. He did not have to do so this way, and I did not expect Him to respond this way. But when He did, I was deeply grateful and humbled by His love.

> **The only life that will produce supernatural, spiritual results is the life of full *surrender* to God's will and way.**

My experience and biblical study have taught me that the only life that will produce supernatural, spiritual results is the life of full surrender to God's will and way. Every other life is a shortcut that will prevent God from blessing us in deep and long-term ways. My grandma died secure in Christ, knowing that her Lord and Savior had blessed her in ways that money, fame, a faithful husband, and other inadequate measures of success could never show. She gave herself to God, and He gave Himself to her.

Are you willing to live at this level of trust?

Do you really believe that God knows best?

Are you willing to surrender to His plan, even if it means you live a life of obscurity and difficulty?

Are you willing, like those in Hebrews 11, to remain true and faithful even if you do not see the fullness of God's promise on this side of heaven?

Chapter 5

The Beginning of Radical Faith in My Life

As I watched my parents live the sold out Christian life, it dawned on me that one day I would have to make a decision about the life I would live. I coasted along through my childhood and teen years caught up in just trying to figure out who I was and what I would do in life. During my teen years I was blessed to sing in a group and travel around the country. We sang in churches, camps, and youth gatherings. I had given my life to Christ as best I understood and really had a serious desire to live for Christ. Because of the group I sang in, I had to express my faith publicly. However, after graduating from high school and getting married at a young age, I found myself drifting away from close communion with the Lord. I ended up managing a small company of about twenty-five employees and thought that I was simply going to make money and "support God's work" as the mission of my life.

In 1988, I was in a motel in Gatlinburg, Tennessee, enjoying a few days vacation with my wife. She was asleep, and there wasn't anything interesting on TV, so I was just lying there in quietness. The Holy Spirit used that silence to get my attention. He began to talk to me.

"Jeff, do you really love me?"

My pat answer was, "Sure I love you Lord."

But He was persistent. "Do you really love me?" As I pondered this question, the Lord seemed to ask another: "Do you love to pray and commune with me?"

As I thought about it I had to say, "Not really."

"Do you love and enjoy my Word?"

I thought about it and had to answer, "No, not really." I also realized that I didn't even enjoy going to church any longer. I was just going out of a sense of moral duty and tradition. I couldn't wait till the services were over, and I surely hoped God wouldn't break in and lengthen the service.

I was at best one of those "lukewarm" Christians Jesus wanted to spew out of His mouth in the Book of Revelation.

I realized in that motel room that I was at best one of those "lukewarm" Christians Jesus wanted to spew out of His mouth in the Book of Revelation. I got down on my knees beside my bed and asked Jesus to forgive me and to begin a new work in my life. I can't honestly say that everything changed instantaneously, but what did happen was a new level of hunger for God. And it did not take long for His plan to begin developing in my life.

Within twelve months of this experience, God called me to attend a Bible college in south Florida. I obeyed and moved there from my home in Indiana. I attended one semester and liked it, but something was still calling me away. As I mentioned earlier, the thought of completely turning over the control of my life to God scared me. I had been around a lot of missionaries who had spent their lives across the planet somewhere. I had also watched my father sacrifice greatly to engage in ministry. I remembered standing outside the parsonage on Wednesday nights when most of the families in the church were going to Dairy Queen. The kids would holler and ask us if we were going, but most of the time we couldn't go because we didn't have 10 cents to buy a Dilly Bar. I had a wonderful childhood and wouldn't trade it for anything, but the Devil was using some of those experiences as a tool against me. I didn't want to be a poor preacher. I didn't want to have to buy my kids clothes at the Disabled American Veteran's store like we had done throughout our childhood. Growing up with eight brothers and sisters meant that people didn't always want to invite us over to their house. Sometimes I felt like we were somehow inferior to my friends who had money, nice cars, and houses. While I was growing up we never owned our own home; we were always living in somebody else's house.

So on February 11, 1990, I found myself sitting in our winter camp meeting at the college I was attending. I had told my father that I would be leaving the Bible college at the end of the year to go to a college where I could prepare to become a lawyer. He gave me what I call a loaded answer when he said, "Son, you do whatever the Lord tells you to do, and I will fully support you."

On that February night, the preacher spoke in a very quiet tone to the 1,500 people in attendance. He talked about fully yielding your life to Christ and allowing the Holy Spirit to have absolute control. I sat through the whole service under a deep sense of conviction. I debated with the Spirit of God. I tried to convince Him that I was just fine in my current state and didn't need to go to that altar. I was worried about my image. Everyone there knew that I was a "fine Christian." I didn't want them to think differently. As I look back on this very important night in my spiritual life, I am amazed at the patience and persistence of the Holy Spirit. I was resisting His call, and yet He kept calling. He could have left me alone as I tried to push Him away, but He didn't because He had a plan for my life. No matter what it took, He was going to lead me towards that plan until I accepted or flat out refused to follow.

As the altar call was given that night, I waited and waited. I continued to resist the voice of the Holy Spirit. I made a deal when I thought the worship leader might be done singing. I said, "If he sings one more verse, I'll go." The Holy Spirit nudged the singer and sure enough, after I thought he was done, he started another verse.

I ended up kneeling at a metal folding chair on a concrete floor. I really didn't know how to pray that night. I started praying in a way I had heard others talk about. I was manually going through a list of things I thought I might need to surrender. I told the Lord He could have my new car. He didn't seem interested. I told Him He could have my new wife. Same response. I went down my laundry list of "things" before God finally whispered into my soul, "Jeff, what I really want is ALL of YOU."

I quickly responded that I was ready to give Him that.

He then zeroed in on one aspect of my heart and life: "Will you surrender your pride?"

"Yes," I replied, "I will surrender my pride."

"I want you to prove it," God said.

I suddenly felt that the Lord was asking me to lie on my face on the concrete floor. In that moment, I couldn't think of a more horrific thing to do in front of that large crowd. No one else was doing anything so "out of order." One voice was screaming inside of me saying, "This is ridiculous. God would never ask you to do something so stupid." But there was another voice speaking tenderly and firmly, "Jeff, show me that you're willing to surrender your pride. Go down."

It felt like an eternity as I wrestled with God at my personal Gethsemane. It was utterly agonizing. Somehow, after a few minutes and feeling like God was saying tonight is the night, I looked up at my father and a retired missionary who were praying over me. I said, "I don't want to be stupid, but **It was truly a concrete way to die to my ungodly pride— a pride that was preventing me from fully obeying God.** I think God is telling me to lay on my face." I think I was hoping that they would save me and tell me that God wouldn't ask that of me. To my disappointment, they just said, "You do what the Lord is telling you to do." Till the last second I was trying to figure out how to lie down on that concrete floor and still look good. I soon realized there was no pretty way to do it. As I was going down, the Lord said put your hands down by your side. It was one of the most helpless positions in which I had ever been in my entire life. Falling on my face in front of hundreds of people who I so desperately wanted to impress was excruciating. I wanted them to think highly of me, but God was asking me to humiliate myself before them. It was truly a concrete way to die to my ungodly pride—a pride that was preventing me from fully obeying God.

I finally obeyed and went down to the floor. I laid face down with my arms at my side. Then, in my humiliation, God brought me back up.

I had never had a great emotional experience with God before that night, and I have had nothing that equals it since. However, on that night, as the Holy Spirit led me through this process of absolute surrender, He also touched me in a physical way with a sense of praise that was overwhelming. I knew that God had accepted my living sacrifice, and I knew that I had reached a level of surrender to God that I had never known before. As a result, my love for God and people and my hunger and thirst after God increased significantly. I also received a call into the ministry a couple of months later. It seemed like God spoke to me and said, "I couldn't trust you with power and influence until I gained full control."

February 11, 1990, was the first night that I really knew what it meant for God to have all of me. Since that night, I have come to many new places of surrender. Daily I must surrender afresh, sometimes in small ways, while at other times a "big surrender" is called for. This new life with God began on that night in 1990.

I am convinced that if I had not reached that place of surrender to God then, I would have missed His will for my life. God has asked me to do so many things that the unsurrendered Jeff would never have done. But in this constant surrender to God's unique and often unorthodox plan, I travel the journey of Radical Faith, doing life His way, not mine. I would not have life any other way.

Only the person who is utterly surrendered to God will live the life of Radical Faith.

Where do you stand? Are you living, on a daily basis the life of full surrender to God? If not, take some time and seek the Lord. He will lead you to a place of surrender. However, you will have to take your hands off your life and yield it to Him. He wants everything—your job, family, money, other possessions, aspirations, dreams—all of it will have to be at His disposal. Are you willing to go there to begin the journey of Radical Faith?

Section 2

A Willingness to Sacrifice and Suffer

Chapter 6

The Unexpected Cost

When most of us became Christians, we didn't know all that we were signing up for. I was blessed to grow up in a world where the ministers preached repentance and restitution and were unafraid to say that being a Christian would cost you everything. I had also read the strong words of Jesus in Luke 14:26-33 that very clearly spell out the cost involved in following Him. However, I still did not fully comprehend what following Christ would cost me. At some point, if we are ever going to live a significant Christian life, we must come to the place where we are willing to pay any price in order to follow and obey the Lord. By the way, the last time I checked, serving the Devil cost a person much more than serving Jesus does.

Not long ago, I received a phone call from a precious young couple, Matt and Ashley, who had been attending the last church I pastored. This couple, though young in the Lord, had hearts that wanted to please the Lord. In this phone call, they told me that their unborn baby had been diagnosed with Trisomy 18 (a serious chromosome disorder) and that their doctor had highly recommended that they end the pregnancy. The doctor had told them that the baby would be severely deformed and could not possibly live long outside the womb. Matt and Ashley had also been told that if the baby lived, it would be in serious pain and would be a great burden to their lives. As I understood it, they had to make their decision by the following Wednesday. The fact that they were calling their former pastor was evidence that they wanted to make the right decision. I gently tried to make them aware of all that was involved in this decision. I, along with their new pastor and a doctor friend in the church, helped them understand that God was the Giver of life; in reality, He was the only one who had the right to take life. Matt and Ashley pondered our advice and made a difficult yet praiseworthy decision: they chose to live by Radical Faith—to obey the Lord and accept whatever consequences came their way.

Matt and Ashley sent me the following letter they wrote to their family and friends:

Dear family and friends,

We are writing this letter from our hearts today, to give you all some insight as to what Matt and I have been feeling since we found out that Emerson has Trisomy 18 and also to help you better understand decisions we have made, and will soon be making, that will impact our family as a whole. Our hope in sharing this with you is that it will give you answers to questions you may have, as well as to offer comfort in knowing how to support us as we continue on this journey of welcoming our precious daughter into the world. We realize that this is a very difficult time, not only for us, but for you as well, and we believe that by expressing how we are handling everything, it will in turn, help you to better deal with it too.

It was the morning of November 8, 2011, and I remember getting the phone call from our doctor's nurse. My blood tests for possible birth defects had come back showing an abnormality in the baby, and they wanted us to come in to discuss what had been found. At this point, so early in the game, at just 15 weeks, we didn't even know if she was a boy or girl yet. All I knew is that I was in shock. As I hung up the phone, I started to make my way back to the bedroom to tell Matt that he needed to stop getting ready for work and start getting ready to go to the doctor's office to discuss what might be wrong with the precious life we created, and so dearly wanted, that was growing inside of me. As I made my way from our kitchen to tell him, so many things were going through my head. Is the baby okay? What could possibly be wrong? Could it be spina bifida? Could our baby have Down Syndrome? It was not until a few weeks later when we realized that we could only have wished for a baby with Down Syndrome. Keep in mind; I had never heard of Trisomy 18, so that never even crossed my mind. I will never forget my walk from the kitchen to the bedroom that morning. Having just been given the gut-wrenching news, I remember stopping in the dining room, not having a clue what may have been wrong, if anything, I placed my hand on my belly and whispered out loud, "Don't you worry, I promise you that I won't let anything happen to you ... Mommy and Daddy love you so much, no matter what."

It was about a month later, on December 10, 2011, when it was confirmed by amniocentesis, that Emmy had Trisomy 18. When we got the diagnosis we were devastated. We decided to meet with our pastor the next day to discuss our news and to try to get some guidance for where to go next. After a good hour of very engaging conversation, Pastor Dave said something that Matt and I found very powerful. He said, "You guys have two choices. You can choose to walk with the Lord and carry her, leaving her fate in His hands, or you can choose to walk without Him (he was referring to terminating the pregnancy). Although God will support you one way and not the other, He will always love you no matter what you decide, but the choice is yours." There was our answer! Termination was not an option for us. At this point, we knew that Trisomy 18 could make us or break us. We had a choice. We could dig a hole and cover ourselves up, isolate ourselves from the world and feel sorry for ourselves, or we could choose to keep our chins up, hold our heads high, and be strong for ourselves, our family and for little Cole by embracing this challenge and looking straight ahead, keeping our focus on God and His will. We ultimately decided to trust God with her life for we knew we had to be obedient to His plan for our family. Matt and I have realized that it is not about our lives here on earth, but it is all about eternal life.

In the beginning, we prayed for three things. We prayed for comfort to accept it, for peace to be able to talk about it, and for strength to get through it. God's grace is amazing as we feel we have been given all three. We've been given comfort simply due to everyone's prayers. We are so blessed to have so many people praying for us and those prayers are being felt daily. As for peace, we have the uttermost peace by knowing that God has called us to be His servant in this, and He will see us through. This is not a surprise to Him. He knew long before we did that we would be in this position today. He chose us because He knew we would walk with Him, and we know that by doing so, it will give Him great glory because it is only His will being done. And as for strength? You know, so many people ask us, "How can you be so strong?" The answer is simple. We are not strong. We get our strength from God. Without Him we could not do this.

Despite the pain over these last few months, that has been so deep because we love her so very much, our faith has grown immensely. Please understand we do not blame

God for Emerson's condition and neither should you. God did not cause this to happen, He only allowed it. There is a reason for it all, and yet we may not ever know the reason, we trust in Him and know that, however difficult it may be, it's the right decision because it's His decision. That being said, it is important for you to know that we are still praying for God to give her complete healing. We are still praying for a miracle, and we know that in order to receive a miracle, we must expect a miracle. We're sure that is what a lot of you are praying for too. However, if it is His will to take her from us prematurely, we will accept it because Emmy already has a secure place in Heaven for all eternity, and we know that we will see her again someday. But, some of the lives that she may touch, and that our story may touch, may not have a secured place in Heaven. We believe that part of her purpose is to bring those who love her, and us, closer to God. If her tender life could bring just one person closer to God, then in our eyes, it was all worth it.

Matt and I refuse to let Emerson's condition destroy us. We are a closer family because of her and feel that we have a stronger marriage having gone through this, as well as a much deeper relationship with Jesus, and we owe it all to Emerson. As difficult as it has been, and is yet to be, we are showing our love to God by learning to accept the possibility of having to completely let her go and give her back to Him if that is what's to be. Emerson has already taught us so much, and we are ever so grateful. She has taught us unconditional love in a way that is unimaginable. Trisomy 18 is just a condition, but Emerson is our daughter, and we love her unconditionally no matter what. At our young age, she has taught us just how precious life is. Most people don't begin to realize this until much later in life or when faced with a terminal illness themselves. But most importantly, Emerson has taught us to always stay strong in our faith and to never give up on the Lord. If He brings you to it, He'll bring you through it. We truly believe that.

We want to remember this pregnancy, and her life, as a happy, loving, bonding time for Emmy and our family. Don't be afraid to talk to us or ask questions. We love to talk about her, and it actually helps us to talk. We've learned a lot about her condition and hope that everything we've shared with you today has taught you something too. Please know, we need our family and friends now more than ever. The future is uncertain for us and our little Emerson, so we will just wait and see what God has in store. He brought us this far, and He's not going to leave us now. He will forever be glorified by our decision to carry Emmy because we were given a choice, and we chose Him. In any event, whether cradled in the arms of Mommy and Daddy here on earth or looking down on us from up in the Heavens as she shows off her wings, she will always be our little angel.

With love,

Matt and Ashley

Little Emerson came into the world a couple of months after this letter was written. I was out of state on a trip, and Matt called to ask if I could come and dedicate her to the Lord. Thankfully, another pastor in town was able to do so. Soon after, Emerson went to be with the Lord.

The decision to place their daughter in God's hands, rather than play God by taking her life, is a beautiful example of Radical Faith and a willingness to sacrifice and even suffer, if that's what obeying God requires. Matt and Ashley counted the cost. They knew that Emerson might require around-the-clock care for all of her life if she survived. Yet, they were willing to pay the price.

Shortly after Emerson's birth and death, Matt and Ashley started the Emmy Lane Foundation to help parents who have suffered the loss of a baby. Over the last eighteen months they have helped numbers of parents during their time of grief and loss. They now realize that their act of Radical Faith is allowing God to use them to impact their world in new and unique ways. Do we really have enough faith in God and His plan to obey Him when it costs us dearly? Matt and Ashley did, and when they are faced with tough decisions later in life, their walk with God through the valley of their child's disorder and death will give them perspective and strength that they would not have had otherwise. They are prepared. Are we?

Chapter 7

The Cost That Benefits

Who wants to suffer? Who wants to give up what they like or love?

None of us do. In fact, we do what we can to avoid suffering and sacrifice. If we could eliminate them from our lives, we would. Life would be so much easier without them.

This desire to make life easy is why people dream about retirement from the first day they start working. They talk about it, plan for it, do their jobs in light of it. Retirement is supposed to bring us rest, relaxation, play, and no more strife, or at least very little of it. Who wouldn't want that? Our own piece of paradise on earth.

Is anything wrong with this desire? In one sense, no. Our desire for paradise is innate within the human soul because we were originally created to live in such a world. Adam and Eve did not have to suffer and sacrifice before they brought sin into their lives and this world. The curse, brought on by sin, is what has produced all of the difficulty in this world (Gen. 2-3). Before the Fall, work was not a bad word. It was, and still can be, a very fulfilling part of human existence. But so many people today do everything in their power to avoid having to face the challenge of working hard. They may even dream about winning big in the lottery, so they won't have to work anymore. This is understandable. There is a vacuum in every human heart that longs for a restoration of paradise—a place where suffering and pain no longer exist, where everyone and everything operates just like God planned. This is what heaven will be like. It will be an incredibly beautiful and peace-filled place. It will be everything our broken hearts have ever longed for.

But that promised place is not ours yet. Until that time, we will know suffering—what the apostle Paul calls "the sufferings of this present time" (Rom. 8:18). And these sufferings are what everyone experiences, Christian or non-Christian, a man or woman of Radical Faith or someone without that level of commitment. All suffer. But not all suffering and sacrifice bring the same results. The suffering and sacrifice that come from rejecting God's plan and purpose are ultimately pointless; they bring no everlasting profit or benefit. Instead, they produce a life of waste and unnecessary tragedy. On the other hand, the suffering and sacrifice that come from the choice to obey God lead to a life of great significance and supernatural impact. Fame as the world knows it may not be a part of this life. But such a life lived is far greater, far more influential and productive, than any life lived apart from God.

Satan has fooled people into thinking that serving him is the easy way and serving God is the hard way. Following God can and will cost us, but that cost is "not worthy to be compared with the glory that is to be revealed to us" (Rom. 8:18). Following Satan, however, is the ultimate bait and switch. He promises ease and pleasure, but in return enslaves, steals, and crushes one's life. I have watched saints and sinners all my life, and I know for sure that the Bible is true when it says, "The way of the transgressors is hard" (Prov. 13:15, KJV). A life lived according to the truth of God's Word will have its challenges and trouble, but the end product will be sweet, healing, and blessed. The life lived in the flesh and according to the evil ways of this world, however, will be full of more trouble than can be imagined and the end products will be bitterness, regret, and brokenness.

> **Following Satan is the ultimate bait and switch. He promises ease and pleasure, but enslaves, steals, and crushes one's life.**

Chapter 8

The Cost That Breaks Us

I learned a long time ago that God's laws were put in place to protect us, not restrict us. I have heard someone say, "You don't break God's laws; they break you!" His laws exist for our benefit. When we break them, we hurt ourselves and often others as well. And the worst consequence of our law-breaking is our own demise. As the apostle Paul tells us, "The wages of sin is death" (Rom. 6:23). Sin produces death in every way imaginable in the life of the rebellious person. When we choose to defy God and live life according to our sinful, fleshly desires, terrible things come into our lives. I can't possibly remember all the stories of utter destruction I have heard in my office as a pastor. From the broken person recounting how their life was great until their parents divorced, to the guilt-ridden lady who thinks she was responsible for her sexual abuse. Sin destroys 100 percent of the time!

You see, God made all the laws in the universe. He made the physical laws, such as the law of gravity, and the moral laws, such as, "You shall not steal" (Deut. 5:19). He also made spiritual laws—laws that have to do with our direct relationship with Him, laws such as, "You shall have no other gods before Me" (Deut. 5:7).

Consider His physical laws. Most people are smart enough to know that you do not ignore or defy the law of gravity. If a person went up onto the roof of a tall building and screamed out, "Law of Gravity, I don't believe in you; you have no control over me; I will do what I want regardless of you," the law of gravity is not going to scream back, "No, you will hurt yourself if you ignore me." That's not how it works. The law is there, and if a person chooses to jump off the top of a building, he won't break the law of gravity; it will, however, break him. And remaining ignorant of the law of gravity will not change its power over you. Even a child too young to understand this law will pay the price for violating it. Physical laws do not discriminate. No matter our age, gender, religious beliefs, national origin, or what have you, when we violate physical laws, we pay a price, and sometimes that price is our very lives.

God's laws exist for our *benefit*.

Now, we understand the physical laws God made much better than we do the moral or spiritual laws. But in reality, when we violate or ignore the moral laws, they crush us just like the physical laws even if we don't know they exist. I have heard a fool or two in my day say something like, "I don't want to know the Bible very well because then I will be held accountable for what I know." That's like saying don't teach me the law of gravity because then, when I fall off a cliff, at least I won't know I'm going to die. Moral and spiritual laws bring with them their own consequences. As Paul warns us, "Do not be deceived, God is not mocked; for whatever a man sows, this he will also reap" (Gal. 6:7, NASB). We sow good or evil. We can uphold God's laws or challenge them. Whichever we sow, that's the crop we will also get.

God said, "You shall not steal," because He knew that no decent society can exist in a world where people cannot hold onto the things they have earned. He said, "You shall not lie," because He knew that in order to have great relationships you must have trust. Such actions as lying, stealing, and committing adultery hurt people. We know what this world is like because that's the world we live in. We have sowed immorality, and we are reaping the wreckage that comes with it. But imagine our world if everyone obeyed just the Ten Commandments. We would have no need of police officers, courts, prisons, armies, and a great deal of other forms of protection and justice-keeping that are standard needs today for maintaining some semblance of law and order.

Sin brings pain and destruction. That's the bottom line. Apart from sin, we would live in a much better world—a world where freedom leads to joy, ever-deepening relationships, rewarding workplaces, dreams imagined and achieved without the losses that so often come with them. But in the world we now have, suffering and loss are characteristic of it. And in far too many cases, these are caused by sin—either ours or someone else's.

Chapter 9

The Half-Hearted Life

The church in America is full of half-hearted Christians. Understand that many of the people who profess to be saved have probably never been saved or are completely backslidden. However, there seem to be many saved men and women who a long time ago settled for a religious life but are in no way living the life of Radical Faith. They are committed to their church, their traditions, and their standards of behavior and lifestyle. Most of them hold strong beliefs in the area of politics and culture. But they are living in the flesh and not the Spirit. They resist every move of God, using spiritualized rationalizations that seek to maintain their entrenched desire to keep everything safe and secure in their life. Many of them hire pastors who are as dead and cold as they are. These are the pastors who tailor their sermons so they won't offend the biggest donors. They wink at sin in the life of believers and leaders because they think their mission is to secure a good reputation for their church and even for Jesus. Some of these pastors even preach it "real straight" if that's what the key leaders of their church want to hear. Whether they believe what they are preaching really doesn't matter. Other pastors compromise by watering down the truth of God's Word. Churches with such leaders and followers rarely produce people of Radical Faith because they are more concerned about living a "holy" version of the American dream than they are concerned about getting on mission with a God who might turn their world upside down.

Half-hearted obedience really amounts to a faith that wears the banner of Christianity but lacks the *substance* of the Christian faith.

What kind of sacrifice and suffering does the half-hearted Christian life produce? First of all, half-hearted obedience really amounts to a faith that wears the banner of Christianity but lacks the substance of the Christian faith. It is Christian in name but not in reality. Hence, it is a "faith" of disobedience, and disobedience always costs us dearly. You may not stand for gay marriage or abortion or some other "big" sin, but if your lukewarm heart allows you to excuse your lack of concern and love for the lost, you are falling far short of God's plan for your life. People go to hell every day because they never met a Christian full of the love of Christ (see 1 Cor. 13:1-3).

If your lack of passion for Christ causes your church to water down the truth, you will actually do what Jesus said the Pharisees did and make a convert twice the child of hell (Matt. 23:15). You will bring unsaved persons into your church, convince them that your brand of Christianity is what God expects, and make them twice as hard to reach with the true gospel. Once we convince someone they are saved when in reality they are not, they are much harder to lead to Christ than the person who is irreligious and knows it.

The half-hearted Christian life also leads to the church fights and splits all of us have seen across the years. My guess is that the majority—perhaps as high as 90 percent—of all church fights and splits have been over issues God is not concerned about. For instance, I heard a story about a group of church members who had the need to put a new roof on their sanctuary. They decided to use shingles but could not agree on the color. After much rancor and nonsense, they came to a genius conclusion: they decided that they would put one color of shingles on one half of the roof, and the other preferred color on the other side. The person who told me this story said that each Sunday the group who wanted black shingles would enter the sanctuary and sit under the black side of the roof, and the group who wanted grey shingles would sit under the grey side. Does anyone honestly believe that the Spirit of God was anywhere near that church?

I've known of church business meetings that actually broke out into fistfights. One lady who was in her sixties told me about a fight in a church that she saw as a little girl. It frightened her so much that she ran out of the church. To this day, she is still traumatized by the event.

Half-hearted Christians end up becoming devoted to the dumbest causes (such as, the color of the paint, the type of carpet, the style of pews or chairs, or who gets a set of keys to the church) all in the name of Jesus. They will gossip about, tear down, and destroy their fellow Christians—all in the name of standing for what is right. In so many ways, they reduce Christianity to something far less than God intended, even to something He would not recognize as Christian, and in the process they often lose their children to this world because their progeny see through the hypocrisy.

Half-hearted Christianity comes at a high cost, as does the life devoid of the faith. Both kinds of life are filled with suffering and sacrifice, but not the kind of suffering and sacrifice that benefit us and others. Rebellion, disobedience … whatever you want to call it … will cost us dearly. But only the life of Radical Faith will produce a harvest of blessing and righteousness through the faithful obedience we sow. Only this kind of life has God's favor. Only this life will reap great rewards even on the other side of the grave. This is the price worth paying.

Chapter 10

The Giver Is Worth It

I remember my father telling me on a number of occasions as I was growing up, "Son, you're never really prepared to serve others until you have suffered yourself." I did not understand what he meant at the time, but his insight sounded wise.

Today, at the midpoint of life, I have a much deeper understanding of what he meant. *Sacrifice and suffering shape us in ways that success simply cannot.* The most dangerous leader on earth is one who has never had to sacrifice or suffer to any significant degree. When I meet arrogant people, I assume they simply haven't suffered enough yet to know their own weaknesses. That great boxer Mike Tyson had it right when he said, "Everybody's tough until you bust 'em in the mouth."

The Bible and numerous other historical sources recount men and women who were willing to pay any price because of their faith in God. Let's take a look at a few of them to see what we can learn about sacrifice and suffering in the life of Radical Faith. In this chapter we'll begin with Abraham.

Abraham and Isaac

This Old Testament story about a father of great faith and his love for his son always tugs deeply at my heartstrings. I cannot imagine Abraham's agony over whether to obey God and sacrifice his son, or whether to disobey God in an attempt to save his son's life (Gen. 22:1-19). I know that Abraham ultimately showed amazing confidence in God and His plan (vv. 5-14; cf. Heb. 11:17-19), but surely there must have been a moment when he thought, "God, are you serious?" Isaac was the promised son. He was a miracle child in every way (Gen. 17:15-21; 21:1-8). How could God possibly ask Abraham to take his life? Like most parents, there is nothing closer to my heart than our two daughters. I never knew how protective I could be until our two girls came into this world, but I now know, beyond a shadow of a doubt, that I would give up my life in a second in order to save theirs. How much Abraham must have struggled!

However, as I have pondered God's command and Abraham's obedience, I have learned that everything we have is a gift from God, and He can take it all away and still be a good God. He was not being unfair when He asked Abraham to return Isaac; Isaac belonged fully to Him anyway. Abraham chose to obey God because he understood this truth, and he knew that if God so chose,

He could restore Isaac's life to him. *Anytime we hold something back from God, we are acknowledging the fact that we think that "thing" belongs to us, not to Him.* I've seen way too many parents hinder their children from following God's call upon their life simply because it would move them out of town. I understand that struggle over letting your children move away. When one of my daughters turned fifteen, she approached me with wanting to go to a Third World country to do ministry, and she would be leaving without me at her side. I said yes, but not without some hesitation, lots of questions, and internal struggle. Now

> **Anytime we hold something back from God, we are acknowledging the fact that we think that "thing" belongs to us, not to Him.**

at nineteen, she wants to go to Afghanistan. That scares me. But I know that she belongs to Jesus, and I trust Him to work His will in her life. I refuse to hold her back from giving her all to Christ.

"Without faith it is impossible to please God" (Heb. 11:6). I think that for Abraham to have obeyed God as he did, especially with his own son's life, he had to believe that God knew best. The act of sacrificing Isaac, the promised descendant, made absolutely no sense from a human perspective. Can you fathom what Sarah would have said had she known what Abraham was about to do? Genesis 22 gives the account of what Abraham heard from God and did, but it gives us no indication that Sarah was brought into the loop. What would the mother of Isaac have done? We can only speculate, but if you are a mother, put yourself in her shoes and ask yourself—honestly, now—what would you have done? Would you have supported Abraham, or would you have fought against him, even kidnapped your son to get him out of harm's way? Sometimes, when God asks us to do something, not even our closest friends and family members will understand. This road of Radical Faith can be lonely at times. I wouldn't be surprised if loneliness is what Abraham felt as he and Isaac were walking together up the mountain to offer a sacrifice that only Abraham knew the identity of. I suspect that had Abraham taken a poll among his family members and friends concerning whether he should obey God—or, for that matter, had even heard from God—he would have been urged away from obedience. In fact, he never even told Isaac what God had called him to do. Would Isaac have gone with his father if he knew that he was the intended sacrifice?

Sometimes, when God asks us to do something, not even our closest friends and family members will understand.

I've met a lot of Christians who use the "wisdom" of others as an excuse to avoid doing what God has asked them to do. There's always some "really spiritual" person who will advise us to walk the road of the flesh rather than the path of faith. Abraham acted by faith, and in this case he did that alone and without seeking outside counsel. Normally, I believe we should seek spiritual counsel before we make major life-changing decisions. However, there are so few people who live this life that often the counsel we receive comes from those who are trying to justify their own lack of faith.

I have learned that most Christians will obey God as long as the cost is minimal, and the way out is clear if something were to go wrong. Only a small percentage of Christians are willing to abandon all for the sake of the call. Abraham, on the other hand, was willing to pay the ultimate price because he knew that God would never ask him to do anything less than what was best for him and everyone else involved.

People have asked me, "How do you know when God is telling you to do something?" My answer is less than profound. I simply tell them that if their heart is fully yielded to God, He is big enough to make Himself and His will clear. We find ourselves in the greatest danger of missing God's will when we are living in any form of willful disobedience. Abraham obeyed God all the way to the point of raising a knife to take his son's life; only then did God show up to point him toward a substitute sacrifice. God wanted to make sure that this miracle boy had not become an idol to Abraham, that Abraham was more in love with the Giver than

> **We find ourselves in the greatest danger of missing God's will when we are living in any form of willful disobedience.**

he was the gift. Abraham passed the test. He kept God first. He remained centered on the Lord over all else. For him, the Giver mattered most and knew best.

Worth Following?

How often do we fall in love with the blessings of God while falling out of love with the Blesser? He gives us position and material blessings, and we wake up one day afraid to lose them. We're so afraid of losing His gifts that we won't invest in His work. Instead, we end up hoarding and protecting to make our life comfortable, easy, safe, and predictable. We won't go on a mission trip because we love our lifestyle too much. We don't want to give up our vacation at the beach for a stint in inner-city ministry or digging water wells and building houses in Third World settings. Some sacrifices for God are, we tell ourselves, simply over the top, too much to ask. But are they really? In light of all God has done for us and all He has prepared for us, is there really any sacrifice too great, any suffering too much, any commitment too demanding? Has He not proven Himself worth following?

I often tell stories of things God has asked me to do in the past. Some of them have been fairly challenging acts of faith. And even after doing them, God will whisper into my heart, "Are you still willing to do it now?" Now that I know the cost, am I willing to still follow Him, even if He calls me to do more of the same?

I heard a story that went something like this. A man came to church almost completely broke. All he had to his name was a one-dollar bill in his pocket. He was very discouraged and feeling hopeless, but at least he had a dollar to buy some coffee after the service. During the service, God asked him to give his last dollar to the church. The poor man resisted a bit but finally removed the dollar from his pocket and dropped it in the offering plate. Later that week he miraculously made a million dollars. The next week he came back to church in a jubilant spirit. He sat down next to a stranger and couldn't help but tell her his story. He said, "Ma'am, you will not believe what happened to me. Last week I came in here with only one dollar to my name. I gave God every dime I possessed and this week He gave me a million dollars." The lady leaned over and said, "I dare you to do it again." Whether this actually occurred or not is unimportant. What matters is what this story illustrates. Are we willing to trust God—over and over again?

In my first pastorate, our little church was facing financial challenges. The congregation had never paid a pastor in their thirty-six-year history—until I became their pastor. Then they started paying me a small salary and rented a tiny little house for my family and me to live in. These commitments were frightening my precious church board.

One night I challenged the faith of the board, at least that's what I thought I was doing. I boldly proclaimed that God would meet our church's financial needs. As I left the board meeting and walked down the hall toward my office, the Holy Spirit began to speak to me. "Do you really believe that I will meet the needs of this church?"

"Yes," I said, "I really believe."

The Holy Spirit said, "Then I want you to take more out of your own pocket and put it in the plate each week."

Now you need to understand that I was not being paid enough to cover my monthly bills. I was teaching outside the church four days a week to supplement my income. And I was putting $25 each week in the offering plate. To my weekly giving, the Holy Spirit said to me, "Double it."

The Spirit's message to me was clear. It was as if He had said to me, "You just made that big speech, now prove your faith." You see, when I challenged the board, I was thinking that God was going to bring new tithe-paying families in to make up the deficit the church was experiencing. I couldn't imagine Him asking me, in my tough financial condition, to make up part of the deficit myself. It's one thing to believe God is going to take out the needed funds from someone else's bank account and quite another when He decides to take it out of yours. And yet, that's just what God called on me to do.

Well, I went home and told my wife what I had heard from God. We agreed that we would follow Him and thereby double our giving. The Lord only asked me to do this for six months—which was quite a stretch for my faith. But at the end of six months, I found that my family and I were better off than when we had started. Encouraged by the results, we kept up our doubled giving for six years. At the end of six years, God allowed me to buy a house for which I got a really good deal. The Lord then said to me, "Figure up what you could sell this house for today and what you would net after closing cost." I did the math. I figured I could walk away with $8,000 at any time if I chose to sell the house I had just bought. The Lord then said, "Add up your extra giving above your tithe over the last six years." When I added up the numbers, the tally came to $8,000 dollars. The Lord said, "See, that's how I do business." Our sacrifice, while faith testing at the time, was matched by God, dollar for dollar.

Two years later, I did finally sell that house. And I netted far more than $8,000. I actually walked away with a gain of $20,000. The Lord said again to me, "See, that's how I do business." We cannot out-give God!

Since that time, I have told this story in numerous public settings, including various preaching and teaching venues. I was so excited about what God had done.

Then one day God said, "Are you willing to do it again?" At this point in my ministry, I had a much better salary, but I wasn't overflowing with cash. I thought I was already being pretty generous by giving $1,200 per year to our missions fund above my other tithes and offerings. Then our church had a missions convention, which stirred my heart. There I decided I would increase my giving by 50 percent over the coming year to $1,800. As I was about ready to fill out the faith promise card, the Holy Spirit said, "Wait, I will tell you what to give." I was a bit surprised, but I waited. I laid the card on my desk, knowing I had about six weeks till our new commitments kicked in. Over the ensuing days, I often looked at that card and wondered how much I would be directed to give. When the time drew near to turn in our pledges, I picked up the card and the Holy Spirit said, "I want you to give $500 per month." I thought, *Lord, that's $6,000 per year!* I knew, though, that this was what God wanted me to do. As I wrote $500 per month on the card, the presence of the Holy Spirit settled down on my office. It was a God moment, and I knew it.

What could God do in this world if *every* Christian was willing to live a life of Radical Faith?

Over the last five years that I pastored that church, I gave $30,000 to missions above my other tithes and offerings. Meeting that amount wasn't easy by any stretch of the imagination, and I don't have a fairy tale ending for you. I just know I obeyed the Lord and exercised Radical Faith for me in that area of my life.

What *could* God do in this world if every Christian was willing to live a life of Radical Faith?

What *would* God do in the lives of Christians if we were all willing to fully obey the Holy Spirit in every aspect of our lives?

Imagine!

Better still, step forward in faith in Him, then watch what amazing things He accomplishes in you and through you. You—and the world around you—will not remain the same. Remember, He is well worth following, even when He requires some sacrifice and suffering.

Chapter 11

Joseph: Radical Faith at Work

Of all the men in the Old Testament, Joseph is the one I perhaps admire most. He trusted God in every phase and circumstance of life, even when most men would have faltered in their faith.

When Joseph was just a young boy, God revealed to him in dreams that he would someday rule over his brothers. Joseph was so confident in God's message that he told his brothers about his dreams. They hated him because of his dreams and schemed to remove him from their lives. At first they wanted to kill him. But they ended up making some money off of him by selling him into slavery (Gen. 37:2-28). Surely at some point Joseph was tempted to back off of his dreams. Maybe it was while he was in the pit waiting to be sold into slavery. Maybe it was when he heard his brothers negotiating the purchase price for his life. At some point he must have been tempted to say, "Hey guys, I just made that up; please forgive me, and let me stay here with you and father." But no, Joseph knew what God had said, and he was willing to pay the price to stand by those dreams.

My father has told me on a number of occasions that "People will forgive you for anything but success." I have noticed that even if you just have a vision for great success, some people will hold it against you. There have been a few times when I asked the Lord, "Why have you asked me to start so many new things?" Sometimes in the flesh, I just wish I could lead one church and one school and not have a vision so huge. The life of Radical Faith is a life that is willing to sacrifice and suffer, if necessary, in order to carry out the call God has placed on our lives. Joseph was willing to stay true to God's dreams for his life, no matter the cost.

One reason so many of us are never used greatly by God is because He knows that He cannot trust us in the smallest areas of life.

After being sold into slavery, Joseph ends up at Potipher's house in Egypt. Potipher's wife tries to seduce him. When Joseph refuses her advances because he cannot imagine "sinning against his God and against his master" (Gen. 39:8-9), she frames him and he ends up in prison (vv. 1-20). I can only imagine how low Joseph must have felt. Here he had taken another stand for God, and again he ends up punished for it. How many of us would still stand by God in this circumstance? Joseph surely had some very discouraging moments. He must have had some long talks with God about what in the world was going on. But at the end of the day, he concluded that God was good and that God had his best interest at heart. So he kept on loving and serving Him, leaving the results to Him (39:21-41:45).

Joseph lived a life of Radical Faith. His dedication shows us what Radical Faith looks like in the everyday grind of life. Radical Faith does not give us a genie in a bottle to grant us all our wishes. This life simply involves remaining faithful and true to God in every circumstance of life. This does not seem glamorous. We like to think of people with Radical Faith as the ones who are well known and successful. In some cases, this is true. But most people living lives of Radical Faith remain out of the limelight, the news, and even our church pulpits and newsletters. We may never learn their name or accomplishments until the next life. Then, however, heaven will ring out their names and their stories will be told. Who they have become and what they have done will be rewarded. And we will stand in awe and admiration and perhaps even shock when we see who receives the greatest commendations.

Perhaps Joseph's greatest exercise of Radical Faith is seen when his brothers are finally bowing before him. It would have been so easy to abandon God in this moment. You see, it's actually harder to obey God when you are successful than when you are living in failure. Here Joseph could have said, "I know what God would have me do, but you know what, I have suffered immensely because of their actions, and they are going to pay." However, he did not choose the path of revenge. He had trusted God in the bad times. Now, with the power of Pharaoh's scepter in his hand, he kept entrusting himself to the One who knew best. Consequently, he treated his brothers with kindness (Gen. 45).

One reason so many of us are never used greatly by God is because He knows that He cannot trust us in the smallest areas of life. If we don't have enough faith in God to obey Him in areas like loving our neighbor as we love ourselves (Matt. 22:39), why in the world would He put us in charge of a lot of people's lives? If we don't have enough faith to tithe $10 when we make a hundred, why would God think He could trust us with a thousand dollars or more? If as pastors we don't have enough faith to thoroughly prepare for preaching when facing a crowd of 40, how could God ever trust us with a crowd of 400 or 4,000? Joseph proved his faithfulness to God long before he held the scepter of power. God knew Joseph could handle the great authority he had been given. God had tested him when he was a "nobody" in this world's eyes, and Joseph was found to be faithful and obedient. If we want to be used by God, we must first be trusted by God. Based on your past and current level of faith and obedience, what can God trust you with right now? A lot or a little?

Chapter 12

The Hall of Radical Faith

Abraham, Isaac, Jacob, and Joseph are just four of the individuals highlighted in the book of Hebrews as models of Radical Faith. If we walked through the other pages of Scripture, we would find numerous others, such as Ruth, Esther, Samuel, Elijah, Daniel, the virgin Mary, Elizabeth her relative, Nehemiah, Isaiah, the apostles—and the list goes on and on—men and women, young and old, who yielded their wills to God and followed Him, even when the odds were stacked against them. In His Word, God has told some of their stories to give us examples of how to live and walk in His light and by His power and wisdom. Let's see how Hebrews 11 describes some of the heroes of faith. As you read the divinely inspired words, think about what these folks did, lost, and gained, and ask yourself if you could be as committed to God as they were.

Hebrews 11:23-12:2

The Faith of Moses

"By faith Moses, when he was born, was hidden three months by his parents, because they saw he was a beautiful child; and they were not afraid of the king's command. By faith Moses, when he became of age, refused to be called the son of Pharaoh's daughter, choosing rather to suffer affliction with the people of God than to enjoy the passing pleasures of sin, esteeming the reproach of Christ greater riches than the treasures in Egypt; for he looked to the reward. By faith he forsook Egypt, not fearing the wrath of the king; for he endured as seeing Him who is invisible. By faith he kept the Passover and the sprinkling of blood, lest he who destroyed the firstborn should touch them. By faith they passed through the Red Sea as by dry land, whereas the Egyptians, attempting to do so, were drowned."

By Faith They Overcame

"By faith the walls of Jericho fell down after they were encircled for seven days. By faith the harlot Rahab did not perish with those who did not believe, when she had received the spies with peace.

And what more shall I say? For the time would

fail me to tell of Gideon and Barak and Samson and Jephthah, also of David and Samuel and the prophets: who through faith subdued kingdoms, worked righteousness, obtained promises, stopped the mouths of lions, quenched the violence of fire, escaped the edge of the sword, out of weakness were made strong, became valiant in battle, turned to flight the armies of the aliens. Women received their dead raised to life again. Others were tortured, not accepting deliverance, that they might obtain a better resurrection. Still others had trial of mockings and scourgings, yes, and of chains and imprisonment. They were stoned, they were sawn in two, were tempted, were slain with the sword. They wandered about in sheepskins and goatskins, being destitute, afflicted, tormented—of whom the world was not worthy. They wandered in deserts and mountains, in dens and caves of the earth.

And all these, having obtained a good testimony through faith, did not receive the promise, God having provided something better for us, that they should not be made perfect apart from us."

The Race of Faith

"Therefore we also, since we are surrounded by so great a cloud of witnesses, let us lay aside every weight, and the sin which so easily ensnares us, and let us run with endurance the race that is set before us, looking unto Jesus, the author and finisher of our faith, who for the joy that was set before Him endured the cross, despising the shame, and has sat down at the right hand of the throne of God."

This is God's Faith Hall of Fame. Many of these believers go nameless here, but their names are written in the Book of Life, enshrined there forever (Phil. 4:3). These were men and women who personify what it means to live a life of Radical Faith.

We discussed Moses earlier, but we didn't talk about his parents. Think about the risks they took to save their son's life (Exod. 2:1-10). They were willing to pay any price in order to do what God wanted them to do. We read in Hebrews 11:23 that it was "by faith" that his parents hid him because they were not afraid of the king's command. For years I have been telling the two congregations I was privileged to pastor that: "Where there is fear, there is a lack of faith, but where there is faith, THERE IS A LACK OF FEAR!" Not all fear, mind you. But a lack of paralyzing fear, a lack of the level of fear that keeps one from doing God's will. Faith—genuine faith—brings with it courage.

The life of Radical Faith, regardless of how it may look on the outside or feel on the inside, has *everlasting* value.

When I spoke at the ten-year anniversary celebration of a school I helped to start, the co-founder who currently leads the school mentioned in her public remarks that in those early days I never seemed to be afraid. The truth is, I did feel some fear, but my faith was much stronger. I was able to overcome my fear because I truly believed that we were going to be successful. My belief was not anchored in me but in the one and only God. I had heard the Lord's voice, so I knew it was His will to start the school and grow it. He guaranteed its success, not me or my efforts. This is why the life of Radical Faith, regardless of how it may look on the outside or feel on the inside, has everlasting value; the eternal, unchangeable God guarantees its value and outcome. And He is never wrong. And He cannot fail.

Chapter 13

Counting the Cost

When you reflect on what so many believers have sacrificed and suffered through the centuries, even paying the ultimate price of their own lives, it becomes clear that God never promised His people that they would have cushy lives. Not even God's own Son lived such a life on earth. The prophet Isaiah even predicted that the Messiah's life would be marked by grief and agony. Here are just some of the things he said about our Lord:

> He was despised and forsaken of men,
> A man of sorrow and acquainted with grief;
> And like one from whom men hide their face
> He was despised, and we did not esteem Him.

Surely our griefs He Himself bore,
And our sorrows He carried; …
But He was pierced through for our transgressions,
He was crushed for our iniquities; …
But the LORD has caused the iniquity of us all
To fall on Him.

He was oppressed and He was afflicted, …
By oppression and judgment He was taken away; ….
(Isa. 53:3-5, 7, NASB).

Did all of this happen to Jesus because He was a wicked man, deserving of judgment? Not at all! Isaiah knew that the Messiah "had done no violence, nor was there any deceit in His mouth" (v. 9). Jesus was "the Righteous One," the very "Servant" of God who would "justify the many," who would "bear their iniquities" (v. 11) though He had no sin of His own to bear. If the Father would not spare His own Son from such hurt, why would He spare us? In fact, the apostle Paul even told us that one mark of us being "fellow heirs with Christ" is that "we suffer with Him so that we may also be glorified with Him" (Rom. 8:17, NASB). Suffering comes before glory.

In a fallen, sin-ridden world, pain and hurt are part of its framework. We cannot avoid them. On the other hand, the kind of sacrifice and suffering that furthers God's kingdom and brings Him and us glory is unnatural in this fallen world. It is a supernatural work with a supernatural impact. It runs against sin and beats it. It marks God's path to victory over the destructive power of evil. In

Christ, this victory is ours, but the path there can be a rough one. This is the path of Radical Faith.

Loss and Gain

Still, knowing what benefits sacrifice and suffering can bring for the cause of Christ does not make them easier to handle. When God birthed the vision of Renewanation in my heart, He warned me that it would cost me dearly. Since we started this new ministry, I have faced intense spiritual warfare, and I have taken some serious hits. However, when I am at my lowest point, the one thing I never doubt is that God is in this effort and that He has called me to lead it. And when I am anxious, even afraid, I find assurance in Paul's rhetorical question, "If God be for us, who can be against us?" (Rom. 8:31). The answer, of course, is that no thing and no one can thwart what God has promised to those who love Him (vv. 28-34). We will have challenges. We will face enemies. We will experience unfairness and injustice. We

No thing and no one can thwart what God has *promised* to those who love Him.

will have setbacks. We will deal with losses, some of which may be deeply painful. But the more we walk with our Lord and Savior, depending on Him and obeying Him, we will find through all of this what Paul found: "I count all things to be loss in view of the surpassing value of knowing Christ Jesus my Lord, for whom I have suffered the loss of all things, and count them but rubbish so that I may gain Christ, and may be found in Him. ... I press on toward the goal for the prize of the upward call of God in Christ Jesus"

(Phil. 3:7-9, 14). Our loss will ultimately be our gain. And what an amazing gain that will be! Full transformation into the image of Christ; everlasting life in and with Christ; an eternal reunion with our saved loved ones; everlasting fellowship with all of God's saints; an evil-free, pain-free life in a new heavens and new earth … and on the list goes (e.g., see 1 Cor. 15:35-58; Col. 3:10-11; 2 Pet. 3:10-13; Rev. 19-22). How can anything here possibly surpass all of that?

In the meantime, though, we must love God supremely and trust Him above all others. And if and when that requires some sacrifice and suffering on our part, so be it. His way is the best way 100 percent of the time. We must commit ourselves to this truth.

Can you? Have you? Do you believe that God's way is always the best way? Is that how you live, or at least want to live? Theoretically, Christians would agree that God's way is best. Practically, however, we often fail to live as if this is so.

When I was writing this chapter, I was frustrated with this life of Radical Faith. Close to a year ago, God asked me to walk away from a safe and secure life. I had just reached the place in my ministry where I had a wonderful salary and a church full of people who loved me and took care of me. One day the church board asked me to follow them out of a board meeting to the front of the church. There, outside the main entrance, sat a brand new Toyota Avalon with a beautiful green bow on top of it. To my stunned face, the board members simply said, "Merry Christmas." Months later a number of people in the church put their money together and bought my oldest daughter a beautiful little sports car to drive to college. Being loved on like this was amazing and wonderful.

Then God spoke to me and asked me to leave it all behind to begin Renewanation.

I don't want to be misunderstood about this. I love this new ministry, and it has grown by leaps and bounds. But while writing this chapter my finance director called and told me that there were not enough funds to give me a full paycheck—again! I really needed the funds. I had bills staring me in the face. I had a daughter in college. I had burned through my financial reserves. I was nearly out of options. I sat back and asked myself, *"Is this work worth the cost? Should I keep following God in it?"* If I answered no, I could walk away and go back to receiving a great paycheck every week. I would no longer wonder if I would be able to make my house payment this month—or any other month. I know, though, deep in my bones that staying the course with God is worth the cost. And He keeps showing me that His way is *always* the best way, though not the easiest way. He meets my needs, not in ways I would expect or even prefer, but He still meets them.

The heroes we read about in Hebrews 11 didn't all have happy endings. As we read, some of them were:

> … tortured, not accepting deliverance, that they might obtain a better resurrection. Still others had trials of mockings and scourgings, yes, and of chains and imprisonment. They were stoned, they were sawn in two, were tempted, were slain with the sword. They wandered about in sheepskins and goatskins, being destitute, afflicted, tormented—of whom the world was not worthy. They wandered in deserts and mountains, in dens and caves of the earth.

They underwent great loss, but God never abandoned them, and their gain has already far outweighed their losses.

Can American Christianity stand up to this kind of example? Unfortunately, no. The American church has wandered far from biblical Christianity. We have mixed materialism with Christianity and created a hybrid that the Holy Spirit wants nothing to do with. We have mixed self-help thinking with the gospel and have created a false view that promises, "If you just do all the right things, worldly success is guaranteed." We shore up this false promise when we invite to speak at our Christian gatherings only those people who are successful in a material, physical sense. "They have the largest, fastest growing church in history" or some other claim to fame. A friend of mine returned from a seminar and said that one of the speakers, a young man, had planted thousands of churches. When you looked at the math, it was clear that this young man had done no such thing. In our craze to be big by the world's standards, we sometimes fall for the absolutely absurd. I, as much as anyone, love to hear men and women speak whom God has blessed and is using for His kingdom work. However, our criteria for judging success are often skewed. Consequently we tend to get drawn to those stories that exude success without sacrifice, discipleship without suffering, missions without hardship, preaching without pain, ministry without loss.

The American church has wandered far from biblical Christianity.

Think about it. How often do we hear from the missionary serving in a Muslim country who has planted a million seeds but has only seen a handful of converts in thirty years? That kind of story just doesn't fit our success mold in America, and it won't raise money for ministry.

My sister Sandy, her six children, and her husband Melvin left the comforts of the USA to go to Ukraine in 1992. The Soviet empire had just fallen, and Ukraine was a mess. After arriving in Ukraine, Sandy and her family were repeatedly robbed; even their vehicles were often stolen.

One night around midnight five masked gunmen came through a window in their apartment. They caught Sandy first, and she started screaming. Melvin came running to her aid from the back of the apartment. The gunmen hit him over the head with a crowbar. Then they put a gun to the screaming baby's head and demanded money from Sandy. Melvin regained consciousness

What *price* are you willing to pay in order to fully obey the Lord?

and fought the gunmen until they beat him unconscious again. In the fight, they knocked over their boy's bunk bed.

After the robbers left, Melvin was lying in a pool of blood on the living room floor. Sandy was naturally in a panic. Being a nurse she feared the worst for her husband. As Melvin started to come around again, Sandy knelt beside him and, like any wife or mother would have done, said to him, "That's it, Melvin! We are leaving this place." Melvin somehow found the strength to say, "No, Sandy, that's just what the Devil wants."

They stayed in Ukraine for eight years. The fruit from their ministry there continues to this day. Many Ukrainians were saved, and many are now in ministry as a result of Sandy and Melvin's work.

This is what the life of Radical Faith looks like. We may not be robbed or physically beaten or have our lives or family threatened, but living for God means obeying Him, even when the cost on this side of heaven is great and grave.

What price are you willing to pay in order to fully obey the Lord?

Chapter 14

Learning From My Parents

I grew up in a somewhat unique home. My parents had nine children, and they were quite conservative in their lifestyle. When we walked into a restaurant, people stared at us like we were walking off the set of *Little House on the Prairie*. Most would ask, "Are you Catholic?" Our pat answer now is, "No, Mom and Dad just didn't have TV." When we were a young family, we would have qualified as low-income. My dad supported us on his pastor's salary.

During one of his early pastorates, he worked part-time for Standard Oil Company. My dad is a talented and gifted leader, so Standard Oil would have been more than happy if he would have given his entire life to their company. He chose not to, however, and he moved to a new church.

Early on I figured out what mattered to my parents. They were sold out to following God's call upon their life. One year my dad preached at more than twenty Monday through Friday revivals while pastoring his church full-time. His heart burned with passion for the cause of Christ. My mother always showed great support for Dad's ministry in spite of the fact that it often meant she had to stay home and carry much more of the family load. This was not always easy for her. I remember watching through the keyhole of her bedroom door as she knelt and prayed over her very hectic life and for her many children.

I have heard Dad tell about the temptations Satan would bring his way in some of those tough financial years. Once while the washer was screaming to be fixed and there was no money to fix it, dad received a phone call from my Uncle Herbert. Uncle Herbert was my Dad's only brother, and he was a self-made millionaire at the time. He had a large highway building company with over a hundred pieces of heavy equipment. He had built this company in spite of the fact that he could barely read or write. He called my dad to offer him a great salary if he would come to Virginia and help run his company. My dad tells how he listened to the washer squeal, thought about all the financial needs he had, and was tempted to walk away from the ministry to a more lucrative life. Thankfully, my dad listened to the Holy Spirit and chose to stay committed to God's call to full-time ministry.

I watched my father make decision after decision that seemed to ignore his need for finances. In 1981, after Standard Oil once again offered him a great position, he chose to accept the presidency of a small and struggling Bible college. For three years he received no salary at this school and had to hit the road to raise funds for his family and the school. As I watched my father, I learned a concrete lesson: *obeying God at all costs is the most important thing you can do in life.* My dad, even in the most difficult of financial times, had a passion for serving the Lord that was beyond contagious. During his ten years as the president of that Bible college, God blessed the school in a great way. Financial stability was established. My dad never got rich there or in any of his other ministries. But the school improved greatly, and the students served and trained there are producing everlasting fruit for the cause of Christ. Our family benefited as well. It was during this time that most of my siblings and I were established in our relationship with the Lord. God certainly rewarded my father's faithfulness.

Obeying God at all costs is the most important thing you can do in life.

As a result of my dad's willingness to sacrifice and even suffer in order to obey the Lord, today eight of his nine adult children are serving in full-time ministry, and the ninth is serving the Lord in the U.S. military.

The life of Radical Faith is not always easy, but it is immensely rewarding. God honors the sacrifices of those who love Him.

Section 3

A Desire to Serve

Chapter 15

Motive Matters

I have really never known any life other than the life committed to serving God and people. I witnessed this life of service growing up, and I made it my own as I merged into adulthood, married, and began raising a family of my own. Even at my birth, serving was exemplified. I was born on a Sunday morning, and as soon as I was delivered, my dad rushed off to preach to his waiting congregation. My second daughter Heidi was born on a Saturday afternoon, and I wrote a whole new sermon that night entitled "You've Got to Be Born Before You Can Start Living." I preached it to my congregation the next morning. Everything in my life has been geared towards delivering the hope of Jesus to hurting people.

This life of service is at the core of the life of Radical Faith.

It flows from a passionate love for Christ first and foremost and then overflows into a passionate love for people. You see, we cannot love God without also loving those He loves. And love produces service—service to God and service to people, His image-bearers (Gen. 1:26-27). I like the little chorus we sing sometimes that simply says, "God loves people more than anything, God loves people more than anything. More than anything He wants them to know, He'd rather die than to let them go. God loves people more than anything." I wish that every Christian would remember that everything we do should be about the people God loves.

The driving motivation in the heart of every Christian should be a tremendous desire to love, serve, and please the Lord and to serve the people Jesus died for.

The driving motivation in the heart of every Christian should be a tremendous desire to love, serve, and please the Lord and a tremendous desire to serve the people Jesus died for.

Jesus' Way

When we look at the life of Jesus, we see a beautiful picture of what our lives ought to look like. The religious elite of Jesus' day could not stand the fact that Jesus hung out with the undesirables. He was always eating with cheaters, adulterers, liars, and anyone else who would listen to Him. He was also open to the religious elite when they approached Him with an honest and open heart.

Jesus' first disciples were not as welcoming as He was; they wanted to turn people away. They tried to send home the hungry.

But Jesus said, "No! Let's feed them." They tried to send away the children. Jesus said, "No! Bring them to me." Jesus was constantly reaching out to lost and hurting humanity. The Gospel of Matthew shows us Jesus' heart for people:

> Then Jesus went about all the cities and villages, teaching in their synagogues, preaching the gospel of the kingdom, and healing every sickness and every disease among the people. But when He saw the multitudes, He was moved with compassion for them, because they were weary and scattered, like sheep having no shepherd. Then He said to His disciples, "The harvest truly is plentiful, but the laborers are few. Therefore pray the Lord of the harvest to send out laborers into his harvest" (Matt. 9:35-38).

Jesus saw the need and did His part to meet it. He had a loving compassion for others.

What drives your life? Are you committed to serving others? Are you motivated with a heart of compassion? Do you love whom God loves?

The Lesser Way

I have met so many in ministry and so many Christians in general who were motivated to offer service to God by something other than a passionate love for God and people. For example, I have known many Christians who were "in it" for what they could get "out of it"—money, recognition, applause, social acceptance, respect, even fame and power. Perhaps this desire to get something is one of the reasons why only 25 percent of all the individuals who start out as pastors retire as pastors, or why so many church members get so angry when their work goes unrecognized. I've also seen and heard from pastors who tiptoe around their church's land mines out of fear that they will offend someone or set off a firestorm of gossip and innuendo. What motivates us matters. I've learned that *if we are not primarily driven by our love for Christ and people, our service to Him and His people will be greatly inferior to what it could be.*

One of my brothers was pastoring a small church. He had not been at this church very long before they decided to hold one of their famous potluck lunches. My brother and the congregation gathered in the church's fellowship hall. When it seemed that everyone was ready to eat, my brother said, "Well, let's pray and eat." Suddenly, some sage of the church quickly approached my brother and said, "We never start one of these meals until sister Mary is here." Well, my brother, not wanting to upset the applecart at his first potluck dinner, decided to wait a few minutes. Finally, after the lady did not show up, my brother chose to go ahead and pray so everyone could eat. Not long after he prayed and everyone dug in, this dear lady walked in the door. She looked around, gasped, and passed out! How dare a church potluck start without her! This lady's motive for serving was far from a love for Christ, much less from a sense of compassion for the needs of others.

Why Serve?

There have been times during my life when my motives for being in the ministry have been tested. One such time occurred in my last semester of Bible college. My wife Michele was pregnant with our first child. I received a call to preach at a little church about ninety miles south of the college. I was told that the church's pastor was sick and that I would only be preaching there for two Sundays. I agreed to fill the need. My first preaching date was the Sunday before Christmas 1992. After the service, I enjoyed a meal with the pastor and his family. Five days later the pastor died.

When I went back to the church to preach a second time, I was informed that their pastor had passed away and then asked if I could come down every Sunday until I graduated

If we are not primarily driven by our love for Christ and people, our service to Him and His people will be greatly inferior to what it could be.

from college in June. A two-Sunday commitment had now turned into a six-month proposal. With family, school, and work, I was already very busy, but I decided to accept the added assignment. I did not know what else to say to this grieving congregation.

After agreeing to preach every week, I began a new pattern. I would prepare weekly sermons after attending classes all week, being a father to a new baby, and working in the school music department. After a couple of months of this routine, I was exhausted. Preparing sermons was hard work on top of everything else I was involved in. I was near the end of my desire and energy to keep up this pace. Now the church board had been asking me to pray about becoming their new pastor, but this church didn't have much to offer financially, and I was already thinking about moving my family so we could be near my parents and our friends. I had reached the point where I wanted to bring my commitment to an early end.

One Sunday morning, as I was driving the ninety miles down I-95 toward Ft. Lauderdale, I was having a serious talk with God. I said, "Lord, I'm done with this. I'm going to find some other 'preacher boy' to take on this assignment. I can't do this any longer." I didn't hear much on the ride down that morning. I think I was too busy running my mouth to hear much from the Lord.

After arriving at the church that morning, I entered the sanctuary and found it empty and quiet. I sat down on the front pew and thought over my sermon. A young lady came up and sat down behind me. We were the only people seated in the sanctuary for about the next twenty minutes. In those minutes I heard much of her broken life story. Now I had been raised in a sheltered Christian home. Frankly, I didn't know the half of what people were going through in this awful sin-sick world. But in this short period of time, this young lady gave me an up close and personal introduction to the horrible realities of sin. She told me about the sexual abuse she endured as a young teenager and her twenty-two years of drug and alcohol abuse that the sexual abuse had spawned. She spewed her hopelessness all over my sheltered little life that morning. Through her, God spoke to me in a way I could not miss. He said to me, in no uncertain terms, "You are going to accept the position as pastor of this church. You are going

Do I *love* Jesus enough to do what He is asking me to do?

to lead this young lady to Me and out of this awful life, and you will reach many others just like her."

This was a watershed moment for me. I had to answer the question, "What really motivates me?" I knew this church had never paid a pastor. I knew this church had no place for me to live. This church was not even a part of my denomination. It was off the radar, unlike a large church that had been recruiting me to come on staff for the previous two years. In that moment, I had to make a choice. Do I love Jesus enough to do what He is asking me to do? Do I love people (like this young lady) enough to accept an assignment that in many people's eyes is not the one I should take?

> In that act of surrender, I chose to *love* the unlovable.

I went back to the college and talked to some of my mentors. They were and are great men, but they did not understand. They basically told me I could not accept that fledgling church because I was destined for leadership in their world, and I could not throw that away. I wanted to please these men. I wanted their approval and blessing. I had to make a decision—a decision only then did I see this clearly: Who would I obey, God or man?

By the grace of God, my desire to please God outweighed my desire to please man, so I chose to obey the Lord. In that act of surrender, I also chose to love the unlovable.

Once I became the full-time pastor of this little church in the summer of 1993, several well-meaning people in the congregation told me not to waste my time with that young lady. They told me that they had tried and failed; she simply would never change. I chose not to follow their advice. It wasn't easy, but within one year this young lady and her husband came to Christ and fought their way out of drugs and alcohol with the help of the Holy Spirit. Today they have eighteen years of being clean and sober behind them, and the husband is a worship leader. Not only were we able to lead this young lady to Jesus, but we also saw scores of her family members come to Christ. Some of her family members would walk into my office and say, "Here's how I see it: if God can save her, He can surely save me."

Any motive less than a deep love for Christ and people would not have allowed me to take this church. Any lesser motive would not have kept me there for seven and a half years. If I had left early or never gone at all, I would have missed out on a great move of God.

Chapter 16

Jesus' Passion for People

Jesus was driven by two great motives: a desire to honor and please our heavenly Father, and a phenomenal love for all of us lost people. We see both motives at work in the Garden of Gethsemane, the night before Jesus faced the cross. Jesus knew exactly what was coming. He understood the price He was about to pay in order to redeem lost humanity. In his own human nature, He asked if there was any other way but the horrible death awaiting Him. As much as He struggled, He still committed His will to His Father, saying to Him, "Not my will, but yours be done" (Matt. 26:39). Even above rescuing humanity, Jesus' supreme desire in life was to please God the Father. And the Father's will, of course, was for Jesus to give His life as a ransom for us all.

Jesus' supreme desire and commitment should be ours as well, for when it is, loving and serving people comes more easily and naturally. *When we are struggling to love and serve people, it is a sure sign that we are struggling to love our Lord.* We are never more like Jesus than we are when we are loving and serving others.

In John 3:16-17, the apostle John tells us why the Son of God came to earth in human form: "For God so loved the world that He gave His only begotten Son, that whoever believes in Him should not perish, but have everlasting life. For God did not send His Son into the world to condemn the world, but that the world through Him might be saved." The Son—Jesus Christ—presents the same message in Luke 15. There He gives us a beautiful picture of God's unswerving commitment to find and restore lost and sinful humanity.

> Then all the tax collectors and the sinners drew near to Him to hear Him. And the Pharisees and the Scribes complained saying, "This man receives sinners and eats with them." So He spoke this parable to them saying, "What man of you having a hundred sheep, if he loses one of them, does not leave the ninety-nine in the wilderness, and go after the one which is lost until he finds it? And when he has found it, he lays it on his shoulders, rejoicing. And when he comes home, he calls together his friends and neighbors, saying to them, 'Rejoice with me, for I have found my sheep which was lost!' I say to you that likewise there will be more joy in heaven over one sinner who repents than

over ninety-nine just persons who need no repentance. Or what woman, having ten silver coins, if she loses one coin, does not light a lamp, sweep the house, and search carefully till she finds it? And when she has found it, she calls her friends and neighbors together, saying, 'Rejoice with me, for I have found the piece which I lost!' Likewise, I say to you, there is joy in the presence of the angels of God over one sinner who repents."

Then He said, "A certain man had two sons. And the younger of them said to his father, 'Father, give me the portion of goods that falls to me.' So he divided to them his livelihood. And not many days after, the younger son gathered all together, journeyed to a far country, and there wasted his possessions with prodigal living. But when he had spent all, there arose a severe famine in that land, and he began to be in want. Then he went and joined himself to a citizen of that country, and he sent him into his fields to feed swine. And he would gladly have filled his stomach with the pods that the swine ate, and no one gave him anything. But when he came to himself, he said, 'How many of my father's hired servants have bread enough to spare, and I perish with hunger! I will arise and go to my father, and will say to him, 'Father, I have sinned against heaven and before you, and I am no longer worthy to be called your son. Make me like one of your hired servants.' And he arose and came to his father. But when he was still a great way off his father saw him and had compassion, and ran and fell on his neck and kissed him. And the son said to him, 'Father I have sinned against heaven and in your sight, and am no longer worthy to be called your son.' But the father said to his servants, 'Bring out the best robe and put it on him, and put a ring on his hand and sandals on his feet. And bring the fatted calf here and kill it, and let us eat and be merry; for this my son was dead and is alive again; he was lost and is found.' And they began to be merry" (Luke 15:1-24).

In these three parables Jesus is teaching us one thing: God is deeply in love with those who are lost and is willing to go to great lengths to find and restore them to the safety of His family. In the parables of the lost sheep and coin, the owners dropped everything and spent as much time as necessary in order to find what had been lost. In the parable of the Lost or Prodigal son, the father (God) shows unbelievable mercy and love towards a son who has wasted so much time and money. The son, like most of us, could not imagine how he could ever be accepted back into the family. He prepared his speech and was ready to be a servant, but the father wouldn't think of it. The father was so overwhelmed with joy that all he could think of was, "For this my son was dead and is alive again; he was lost and is found" (Luke 15:24).

God is deeply in love with those who are lost and is willing to go to great lengths to restore them.

If you are reading this book and you feel estranged from God, meditate on the truths of Luke 15. Right now, God the Father is waiting for you to come home. No matter where you have been or what you have done, God will embrace you and forgive you if only you will come back to Him. Do you feel His call, His tug? Surrender to Him. Let Him renew your life today.

On Mission with God

When Jesus came to earth, He set aside more than we can possibly imagine. He took on the form of a man for thirty-three long years. He submitted Himself to the cruelty of the human race and died the death of a criminal. As He was hanging on the cross and listening to the hatred and mockery spewing out of the mouths of the Roman soldiers, He cried out, "Father, forgive them" (Luke 23:34). This is the ultimate picture of unselfish, unconditional love.

Imagine what God could do in this world if those of us who call ourselves Christians were as committed to people as He is?

Imagine what God could do in this world if those of us who call ourselves Christians were as committed to people as He is?

Not long ago, I was privileged to preach for a weekend at a small church in Louisiana. I didn't know the pastor or any of the people, but I felt led to accept their invitation to speak. As I preached a sermon on the opening night entitled "Why Have We Struggled to Reach Lost People?" I wasn't sure how this was going to be received. Sometimes I have preached in places and challenged people to love and reach the lost, and they simply haven't wanted to hear this message. They didn't want to be confused with the facts of the Great Commission. However, at this particular church, I could tell God was up to something. Over the course of the weekend, He moved, and the people seemed to greatly desire the truth I was sharing.

Not long after I closed the meeting, the pastor called me. He told me that two of his lay members, a man and a woman, had called him wanting to start prayer meetings for the lost. They followed through, and God led them to reach out to their community in a new way.

Soon after that, over forty new families came to their church for a fish fry and block party. The following Sunday four new families showed up for the Sunday morning service.

As I am putting the finishing touches on this book, I happen to be speaking at this church once again. On my first night back I met a fine young boy named Iian. Iian and his mother came to the fish fry and then began to attend the church. The Lord prompted the pastor there to offer this fifth grader a scholarship to their Christian school. God is transforming Iian's life and the life of his family through this church and school and their new vision for reaching out to their community. This church was in need of a fresh move of God, and God is now blessing because they have made a new commitment to loving the people in their community for whom Jesus died.

If we want the blessing of God on our lives and ministries, we must be involved in things that God is involved in and excited about. Here in Luke 15 we are told in no uncertain terms that all of heaven breaks into celebration when one sinner comes to repentance. *When we as Christians get on mission with God and begin to love those Christ died for, God gets on mission with us and great things begin to happen.*

If you give yourself to the life of Radical Faith, your ultimate motivation for service will be your deep love for Christ and your passion for the people He loves.

Chapter 17

Loving the Unlovable

Not long after I started preaching at the little church in Hollywood, Florida, I heard about a weird and scary man who lived next door to the church. His name was Gus. The older people in the church were petrified of him. He would stand outside the church as people came out and cry out, "I am god!" Most of these precious older saints were waiting for a lightning bolt to strike. Gus had a terrible hatred for organized religion, so he made it his mission to harass anyone involved in it. He would even bring his pit bulls onto our unpaved parking area and allow them to relieve themselves there.

I decided rather quickly after moving into Hollywood that I would no longer allow Gus to use our parking lot as a dumping area. I was ready to call the police to come and stop him. But the Holy Spirit whispered into my heart, "That's one way to stop him, but there's a better way." It took me just seconds to figure out that the Holy Spirit wanted me to show Gus love and kindness, and that would be the more effective way to stop his bullying. I listened and began reaching out.

I met Gus' girlfriend first. Gus was about sixty, and Cindy was around half his age. Cindy came walking down the sidewalk one day, and I greeted her. "Hi, I'm Jeff, the new pastor here."

She said, "I don't talk to pastors!"

I was a little surprised at her response, but I quickly said, "Well, in reality, I was introducing myself more as a neighbor than a pastor."

"Well, I like being neighborly," Cindy responded.

"Alright," I said, "let's just be neighbors."

On another day shortly after this meeting, Gus came down the sidewalk. We introduced ourselves, and then he quickly told me that Jesus Christ was a SOB! He went on to say that he was a part of the anti-Christ and that someday he would unmask Jesus for the fraud He was. "Welcome to south Florida, preacher boy!"

I was stunned by Gus' language. I couldn't think of anything I had learned in Bible college that told me how to deal with an antagonistic individual like this. Somehow I kept my composure and didn't punch him. I stayed kind toward him even though it was quite some time before Gus stopped being totally obnoxious. Then one day I noticed that his dogs were no longer making deposits on our parking lot.

Early on I realized that God wanted me to build a friendship with this angry, hate-filled man. He was so different from me that I truly had a hard time when I saw him coming. It got to the point where he would rush down to talk with me as I pulled into the church parking lot. He would write long letters to me explaining his beliefs. At some point he began to take a liking to me. At the close of our conversations, even strongly disagreeable ones, he started telling me that he loved me. I would say the same to him. Often when I would stump him, he would spin around and say, "We get more done in silence," and then he would walk away.

One day, after months of begging me, I gave him one hour to try and convert me to his belief system. We went inside the church and he sat on the front pew while I pulled up a folding chair. He spent one hour or more telling me much about what he believed. He told me about his past lives and the spirit guides who had taken him back to them. He told me that if I didn't "get this," I would come back in a lower life form in the next life. He told me that heaven to him was finally reaching the sun, and then absolute nothingness would take over. Finally, after about an hour, I told him it was my turn. I then took a serious amount of time and shared the Christian faith with him.

At some point in one of these deeper conversations, I asked him what was the worst thing that would happen to me if I failed to "get it." He said, "Well, you'll come back in a lower life form, but you will get chance after chance until you get it." I then told him about the worst thing that would happen to him if he didn't come into a relationship with Christ. There were no second chances after death; just misery and everlasting separation from the Source of all goodness and joy. Clearly, if Christianity was true, the stakes were much higher for him rejecting Christ than for me rejecting his belief system.

We built a relationship for six years. It became very friendly in spite of his continued insistence that I learn to follow his beliefs. I shared Jesus with him through my kindness and love and a thousand other means. I really believed that if I loved him enough, he would get saved. In fact, that was the deal I had with God. My love in exchange for Gus' soul. At least, that's what motivated me.

One day Gus' girlfriend Cindy came down to the church in a panic. She told me that Gus had just learned that he was dying with lung cancer. I went straight to his apartment. On the way, the Holy Spirit spoke to me: "Tell Gus that you and the church will care for him during this battle with cancer." I walked into the apartment, and Gus embraced me, cried, and told me that he had the power to heal himself. I told him I loved him and that we in the church would do anything we could to help him through this difficult time.

Over the next few months, I watched Gus die. Every time I would tell him that we were praying for him, he would simply tell me not to waste my time. He would then say, "If you want to send positive thoughts and energy my way, that's fine, but there is no God, so don't waste your time praying."

I was getting desperate. I leaned on the deal I thought I had with God: If I loved Gus enough, God would save him. I thought I had done this. I had invested six years into this man, and I desperately wanted this relationship to have a happy ending.

Over the final weeks of Gus' life, he told me two things that stand out. One day as I was standing at his bedside, he looked at me and said, "I sure hope the universe will be fair to me when I die." I told him he didn't have to hope, but he could know what was going to happen because of Jesus. He did not respond positively. Later, the last time I remember seeing him, I told him the church had been praying for him that night. He looked up and said, "Whatever works, Jeff, whatever works."

Gus finally died. As far as I know, he never accepted Christ. I was out of state when he slipped out of this life, so I wasn't able to attend his funeral. When I got the news of his death, I was so upset. I pretty much asked the Lord why Gus did not get saved. I had invested all this time and energy in this man who cursed God's name repeatedly, and this is how it ends? As I was praying and pondering, the Lord spoke to me: "Jeff, this was as much about you as it was Gus. You needed to learn to love someone whom you would never have associated with. You needed to learn to love people, wicked people, unconditionally."

Lost people really do *matter* to God, which is why they must matter to us.

Gus taught me anew that lost people really do matter to God, which is why they must matter to us. Whether they come to Christ or not is not up to us; it is not our call to make. What we are called to do, however, is to love them and serve them no matter the outcome. That's what unconditional love does. That's what it is all about.

The life of Radical Faith took me far out of my comfort zone. God asked me to show unconditional love to an obnoxious human being and treat him with the love that led Jesus Christ to the cross to die for him.

We're so good in the church at hiding behind our four walls and demonizing all those bad people out there. It's easy to dislike someone you don't know. But when on this journey of Radical Faith God says, "Go and love them," everything changes.

Some Christians never touch the lost because they refuse to exercise enough faith to get out of their little box. That was my inclination too. But through Gus, I learned that when people figure out that you really love them—not that you love them so you can pad your church numbers or notch another baptism, but that you really love them, unconditionally—they will soon love you and often come to love your Jesus.

Jesus was willing to go to great lengths to find and restore lost humanity. How far are we willing to go?

Chapter 18

Neighbor Love

God has always asked me to build strong relationships with my neighbors. Usually, I have tried to find some way to serve them. I have bought the needy ones food and given them money, and I have mowed more lawns than I can remember. My acts of love and service towards them have always broken down the walls in spite of the fact that most of them thought I was expecting something in return. Once they figured out that I didn't want anything from them, they were amazed, and many of them have eventually given their lives to Christ.

In 1996 we moved across town in Hollywood, Florida. I was hoping to move to a little better neighborhood since we now had a four-year old and a six-week old. Not long after moving into the new house, I noticed that a rather rough looking neighbor lived behind us. He had a ton of tattoos, and almost every night he and some buddies would get drunk in his front yard. My honest response was, "Not again!" I was hoping for some nice Christian neighbors or at least people who seemed to have their life together. That's not what I got. But I knew immediately what the Holy Spirit was nudging me to do, so I went over and introduced myself.

It didn't take me long to realize that my new neighbor, Jackson, was a broken man. I discovered that he was thirty years old and had very little hope in life. One night, as we were talking over the fence, he just blurted out, "I'm either going to get my [expletive] together or I'm going to kill myself just like my mother did." He then went on to tell me how he found his mother in a pool of blood when he was only six years old. She had slit her wrist. This young boy dragged his mother's body into her bedroom so his little brother would not see her. "Before that day," he said, "my life was great, but ever since that day, my life has been hell."

I had no doubt that Jackson was serious about taking his life, so I asked him if we could sit down and talk about Jesus. He said we could a few nights later. I asked Jackson to try to stay sober for that one night, and he agreed.

I walked into his rough little house on the night we had agreed to meet. I sat on a broken down old couch, and he sat in a chair across the room from me. His little dog seemed possessed as it ran circles around me. I was hoping and praying that somehow that dog would disappear, and suddenly it did. Jackson was very nervous as I began to share Jesus with him. He didn't seem to know much about Jesus or the Christian faith. A few minutes into our talk, he stopped me and asked me a question. "Jeff, do you think it would be okay if I just drank one beer while you talk?" He assured me it wouldn't get him drunk and impair his ability to listen to what I had to say. I told him to do whatever he needed to do in order to be able to best hear what I had to say.

He assured me that one beer would calm him down, and it did. So he drank his long neck Budweiser while I told him about Jesus.

> So he drank his long neck Budweiser while I told him about Jesus.

As I was talking in this setting (and in others like it), Satan would often slip in and say to my mind, "Look where you're at. Look where God has placed you. Is this really where you want to be? None of those people you grew up with in the north even know what you're doing anymore. You could be up there pastoring some recognized church and building a name for yourself." As Satan would whisper that into my heart, the Holy Spirit would just as quickly say, "There's no one on earth more important than this desperate soul sitting before you. If you will be faithful to him, I will be faithful to you."

At the end of my presentation of the gospel that night, Jackson said he would like to give his life to Jesus Christ. I led him through a prayer of repentance, and he asked Jesus to become his Lord and Savior. Evangelism doesn't always produce results this way, but God knew Jackson needed a miracle, and He gave him one.

From that night on, Jackson never touched another beer. He was instantaneously delivered from the power of alcohol and many other vices. His countenance changed, his appearance and attitude changed … his whole life changed. He ended up getting a much better job. He was also blessed with a sweet and loving lady who came into his life. God showed up big time and saved a young man from a life of misery.

Jackson moved away after about a year and a half. I lost touch with him, but I know he will never get away from the power of a transforming God. I am so glad that God filled my heart with a passion to serve Him and those He died to save.

Chapter 19

A True Servant's Heart

Most of the people who know me also know my great friend Dan Coy. Dan and I have been friends and ministry partners for a lifetime. We first started traveling and singing together in high school and college, and then we spent most of the last twenty years working together in pastoral ministry. I know of no other person who personifies more than Dan what it means to love Christ and people.

One of the beautiful things about Dan is that he never writes anyone off. He doesn't care what your religion is or your education or anything else. He always believes something good is about ready to happen in your life and that eventually you will embrace Jesus.

A few years ago, Dan first started talking to me about a guy named Brian. He said, "Brian gets nervous when I start talking about God, but one of these days he's going to come to Jesus."

Eventually, I was introduced to Brian. Immediately I knew why Dan liked him so much. He was an ex-marine who had this great outgoing and friendly personality. Brian handled a couple of mortgage deals for me, and through that we became friends, but we never got very far when it came to Jesus. For a number of years Dan kept building and strengthening his relationship with Brian. But Brian never accepted an invitation to come to church, and he stayed away from religious talk as much as possible. As you might have guessed, Brian's reluctance did not deter Dan.

Finally, one Tuesday morning, Dan ran into Brian at a business meeting. He looked deeply troubled. He pulled Dan aside and told him that his wife had just thrown him out of the house. This devastated Brian. Dan called me and asked if there was any way I could meet with Brian in short order. "Yes," I said. Brian later showed up at my office.

When he entered, I could tell that he was a dazed and confused man. To say he had just received his wake up call would be a huge understatement. I asked him to tell me what was going on, including why his wife had thrown him out of the house. As best a man could, he told me his side of the story. He could see very little reason for his wife to be this angry with him. I then proceeded to ask him a number of questions.

After about an hour of our talking, I gave Brian my conclusion. I told him that his wife had every reason to ask him to leave, and he deserved what he got. Of course, this was not what Brian hoped to hear. He later testified before our entire congregation that he thought I was going to show him sympathy and give him some words of encouragement. However, he told the congregation, in these exact words, "Pastor Jeff kicked my butt!"

I wasn't sure whether he was going to get up and walk out or start telling me off. As we continued to talk, the presence of the Holy Spirit settled down on us and Brian began to break. Before long, he was praying a prayer of sincere humility and repentance and asking Christ to forgive his sins and come into his life. In a little over an hour, God took a man who had no clue who he really was and shined the light of truth into his soul.

God took a man who had no clue who he really was and shined the light of truth into his soul.

As Brian left my office that day, I knew the road ahead would be long and hard and that his wife wasn't going to buy his testimony right away. When growing up, his wife had seen a lot of religious hypocrisy. She was far from the Lord at this time. However, that didn't stop Brian from calling her and telling her that he had gotten saved. She simply said, "I sure hope your next wife enjoys your change." Again, Brian was devastated. He called me and told me what she had said. I told him to be patient because there was no way she would believe him until she saw a changed life.

Within a couple of months I noticed a blond-haired lady sitting next to Brian in church. One day I received a card from a lady named Christy who turned out to be Brian's wife. She simply wrote, "Pastor Jeff, thank you for giving me my husband back."

In the years since, Christy has fallen in love with Jesus and hurting people. She has been on multiple mission trips and works every week to bring children and teens to church from a local government housing project. God set Brian free from the vices that were destroying his marriage. Today he shares his testimony wherever he goes.

None of this would have happened if it had not been for Dan Coy's love for Christ and his unconditional love for people.

Chapter 20

Putting Love to Work

Not long after I started pastoring the church in Hollywood, Florida, I was leading about twelve to fourteen new converts in a Bible study every week. I love new Christians because they are game for just about anything. Valentine's Day was quickly approaching, and I had heard about a pastor named Steve Sjogren in Cincinnati who was showering his community with acts of kindness. Inspired by that, I decided to buy several hundred roses to pass out to the families surrounding our church. I asked all the new converts if they would like to help me with this exciting project. They all agreed! They hadn't yet learned you were supposed to be afraid of reaching out to the community. They were actually gung-ho. We prepared the roses together. We stapled a card on the wrapping paper that simply said, *"We hope this act of kindness brings light into your day and shows you that we care and God loves you, no strings attached."* On the back of the card we had our church name and a statement that said, "If we can ever be of service to you, please feel free to contact us."

The streets surrounding our church were not the friendliest streets in the world, especially after dark. But that didn't stop our team of new Christians since many of them had only recently been delivered from drugs, alcohol, or some other vice practiced on those streets.

We received an overwhelming response from the community.

The next Sunday morning a young lady named Susan showed up at church and told us her story. She said that on Valentine's night she had been very sick and ended up in the emergency room until about three in the morning. When she finally got back to her apartment, she found this beautiful rose and card lying on her front porch. I believe she said this was the first rose she had ever received on Valentine's Day. She was so moved that God would think of her that she came to church and gave her life to Christ. Shortly after her conversion, I ended up leading another new converts class in her little apartment.

We had so much fun showering our community with unconditional love that we did it over and over again. In the seven and a half years we were there, we gave gifts to thousands of individuals and families, and many people were saved as a result. Love is powerful! So is serving others out of love!

I often told my congregations that people will not believe that you really love them until you have sacrificed something precious for them. The gift of sacrifice might be giving up some time or money or a promotion at work. Whatever the gift, it must be genuine—in other words, selfless, not selfish. If we only help people when there's something in it for us, that's not an act of personal sacrifice but of hoped-for gain. Authentic Christian love and service are done for others. Period. No ulterior motives involved. Nothing for self-sought. If we ever hope to really win the hearts of people for Christ, not for our own benefit, we must love and serve them unconditionally.

> **People will not believe that you really love them until you have *sacrificed* something precious for them.**

Over and over again through the years, God has asked me to serve my neighbors. On one occasion He asked me to take in our neighbors' trash cans every week, but not to do it when they were around to see who was doing it. I did this for several years. I'm not sure if they ever figured it out, but they ended up loving our family, coming to church, and getting saved.

Love and service to others breaks down a thousand barriers. People are starved for love and kindness in this dog-eat-dog world we live in. I would often show up at a door with a gift and immediately whoever answered the door would say, "No thank you, I don't want to buy anything." I would quickly say, "I'm not selling anything; I just wanted to give you this gift to show you God's love." They would look stunned, as if I was trying to scam them in some way. But as soon as they believed that I was just there to show them love, they would melt. Often, I would have one of my daughters with me to hand the gift to the person. This always helped to break down the barrier.

When we sell out to Jesus and decide to live the life of Radical Faith, we are selling out to serving people, the very ones for whom Christ died. The life of Radical Faith always leads us to the hurting and the needy. A self-centered life and Radical Faith cannot co-exist.

Practicing Love Toward Our Neighbors

Here are some down-to-earth ways you can show Christ's love to your neighbors:

1. Look around this week and see what you can do in a physical way to help someone who is not a Christian. Cleanup someone's yard, shovel their snow, find a friend's car that needs some maintenance and pay for it, get a shut-in out of the house for a while, take a hurting family some food, etc.

2. Hold a neighborhood carwash and wash all your neighbor's cars at no charge.

3. Take some flowers to someone who seems lonely or is going through a difficult time.

4. Seek reconciliation with any neighbor with whom you have had a problem.

5. Find out when your neighbors' birthdays or anniversaries are and get them a card.

6. Smile and wave at every person you meet in your neighborhood this week. Make it a habit—and practice CPR on those who faint when you do it!

7. Ask God each day to give you a deep love for the unsaved around you.

8. Follow the leadership of the Holy Spirit as He guides you to love others.

9. Memorize Luke 10:27—"So he answered and said, 'You shall love the LORD your God with all your heart, with all your soul, with all your strength, and with all your mind,' and 'your neighbor as yourself.'" Then find at least one new way each week for a month to make this truth felt to anyone who crosses your path: for example, gently and respectfully share your faith; give something of yours to someone who needs it more; converse with someone with no other goal than to learn more about that person and their passions; write someone an encouraging note; give some of your time and talents to a community service project or a community-oriented ministry.

As you lovingly serve others, watch what amazing things happen, and then thank God for the results.

Chapter 21

Beyond Our Comfort Zone

Like anyone else, I can be finicky and fearful. I like certain foods prepared in specific ways. I wash my hands a lot because I think about little germs that might be on them. I grew up scared to death of nursing homes and funeral parlors. I had to go to many nursing home services with our church growing up, but the whole time I was simply trying to avoid contact with anyone or anything there. I hated the smells, and I was thrilled as soon as we finished the last hymn, so I could leave.

God has a way, though, of forcing us to face ourselves. With me, He did this through calling me to be a pastor. I quickly learned that in order to obey Him and live the life of Radical Faith, I was going to have to love people so much that I would be willing to face down my natural fears and instincts. God didn't wait long to challenge me. As soon as I graduated from college and took my first church, I had to confront my fear of preaching a funeral. I was more afraid of this possibility than any other aspect of being a pastor.

This fear may sound strange to you, but I came by it honestly. My dear grandfather was terrified of the dead and dying, and he passed his fear on to me. In fact, I was so turned off by funeral homes that when I would drive by one I would literally point my hands and feet in a direction away from the funeral home. I couldn't stand to look at one or even think about one. And God called me to be a pastor!

One day, shortly after I took my first church, I decided that I would meet this fear head on. I stopped by a local funeral home and asked to meet with the home's director. A sharp young man came out, and I told him that I was a new pastor in town and needed to learn something about funeral customs in their area. He was so kind to spend three solid hours with me. He decided to show me every nook and cranny of his funeral home. The whole time I was in shock. I knew I was in big trouble when he picked up a phone and called down to the "Preparation Room." He said something like, "I have a new pastor here. Is it okay if I bring him down?" He took me down some stairs into a basement area. He opened a door, and we walked down a narrow, cold hallway. I knew this was not good! We turned a corner, and I saw three guys standing about ten feet away with big grins on their faces. I think they knew they had red meat on their hands. I glanced around and suddenly noticed that about six inches from my left elbow was a bald head. As I got my bearings, I saw several bodies spread around the room. The undertaker then said, "Would you like to see the embalming room?" I had determined that I would not turn him down on anything he offered, so I said, "Yes." As we entered the embalming room, they had a lady on the table whose face was totally blue. To me she looked like something I had seen at a haunted house. I felt myself getting light headed; I thought I was going to hit the ground. My tour guide looked at me and said, "Are you okay?" I managed to eek out a yes. He then asked me, "Do you want to go?" I quickly said, "YES!" He was then so kind to take me to the crematory. As we walked in, he told me that they had a body in the oven, and then he showed me the remains of about five other bodies. As I finally left the building, I didn't have much of an appetite. On the other hand, I had faced my fear—with God's gracious help.

I can now do funerals and focus on ministry without having to deal with a fear. If I had not been sold out to serving Jesus and people, I would have avoided dealing with the dead. But I wanted to please Jesus, and I loved people enough to step out of my comfort zone.

I've met a lot of Christians who tell God what they will and will not do. Some are petrified of talking to an unsaved person about Christ. Others refuse to get up in front of a crowd and speak. Others won't go on a mission trip because of some fear it produces. Listen, if we want the supernatural success of God in our lives, we must love Him and

If we want the *supernatural success* of God in our lives, we must love Him and people enough to do whatever He asks us to do, even if it freaks us out!

people enough to do whatever He asks us to do, even if it freaks us out!

You still won't catch me hanging out at funeral homes for the fun of it, but God delivered me from my worst fears. Of course, dealing with death involves dealing with the dying and that I learned to love. I can honestly say that I have been honored to be at the side of many a dying person. One of these was a man who at first really didn't want anything to do with me or my faith.

Am I Really Holding This Pan?

Not long after I moved to Hollywood, I needed someone to put some bars on my church office windows. We hired a company, and they sent us a man named John Smith to do the job. At this time John was in his late 50s, I think. And he looked like he had lived out in the sun for a lifetime. He was not at all interested in church and was only nice to me because he had to be.

A few days after he finished the job in my office, I saw him sitting on the front porch of an apartment right down the street from the church. I pulled my car into a parking space and jumped out to greet him. He wasn't all that happy to see me; neither was his girlfriend, Pauletta. I continued to stop in and talk to him from time to time. He eventually started telling me that someday he was going to visit our church, but he never did. One day I noticed that his apartment was empty. I was saddened because now I had no way of contacting him. I had no idea where he had moved.

One night while passing out gifts, my wife and I stumbled upon his new house. I was so excited to see him that I told him that he would never get away from me again. I didn't know how true that statement would be. John and Pauletta had moved close to the church, but they still did not attend.

One day the phone rang and on the other end was Pauletta. She said, "Pastor Jeff, you need to go see John at the hospital." I quickly enquired about what was happening, and she informed me that he had an inoperable brain tumor that was going to take his life shortly. I went straight to the hospital. I walked into John's room, spoke a few words, and then asked him, "John, are you afraid?" He looked at me with a tough guy face and said, "No, I'm not afraid." Then he burst into tears. I talked to him about Jesus. He asked, "Why would He want anything to do with me? I left Him sixty years ago." I told him the story of the thief hanging on the cross. After that John prayed and asked Christ to forgive his sins and come into his life. The change in John was beautiful.

Many Christians miss out on great opportunities simply because they won't allow God to lead them out of their comfort zones.

He and Pauletta began coming to church every time John felt well enough to attend. Then one Saturday afternoon I had the privilege and joy of marrying these two. This was one of the most memorable ceremonies I have ever performed.

One day I was at John's house when he was feeling very sick. We were sitting on his front porch, and he said he needed to throw up. Somehow, the right thing to do was for me to hold the pan while he filled it. I couldn't believe I was actually doing this. It went against everything in my being. The sight, the smell, the sound … everything about it would normally have grossed me out so badly that I would have thrown up too. But it was different on this day. My love for John and my passion to serve this dying man far outweighed any inhibition I had. I felt honored to hold the pan.

Today John is in heaven, and I have no regret that I chose to love him to Jesus.

When I sold out to Christ and agreed to live the life of Radical Faith, I stopped telling God what I would and would not do. Many Christians miss out on great opportunities simply because they won't allow God to lead them out of their comfort zones.

Chapter 22

Loving Fellow Believers

This love and passion for people is not just for those outside the church. It's also for our brothers and sisters in Christ. Jesus said, "A new commandment I give to you, that you love one another; as I have loved you, that you also love one another. By this all will know that you are my disciples, if you have love for one another" (John 13:34-35). How many church problems could have been avoided throughout history if Christians had loved each other like Jesus instructed us?

The life of Radical Faith is a life of radical obedience to all of Christ's commands. If we really trust that Christ knows best in every area, then we won't pick and choose which commands we will obey. In this "new commandment" Jesus gives us in John 13, we are instructed to love our brothers and sisters in Christ just like Christ has loved us. That is a high calling. He loved us enough to leave everything and come down into the muck and mire of our world. He got involved in our mess. He slept in our houses and ate our food. He took our sin upon Himself and died our death.

This kind of love requires our involvement in the lives of fellow Christians. We're not to be nosey but sensitive, not gossips but helpers, not self-appointed critics but discerners, not authoritarian masters but servants. And none of this can occur if we strive to live as "Lone Ranger" Christians—off doing our own thing, separating ourselves from the life of the local church. How can we fulfill this command to love each other if we are totally uninvolved in each other's lives? The life of Radical Faith is a life of submission to God and to the Body of Christ. We accept what God has said and obey Him because we trust that His plan works better than ours.

Look at just a handful of the many passages where we are given God's expectations for how we are to love and care for each other.

> "Since you have purified your souls in obeying the truth through the Spirit in sincere love of the brethren, **love one another fervently with a pure heart**" (1 Pet. 1:22).

> "And above all things **have fervent love for one another**, for 'love will cover a multitude of sins'" (1 Pet. 4:8).

> "Owe no man anything except to love one another, for **he who loves another has fulfilled the law**" (Rom. 13:8).

> "And may the Lord make you **increase and abound in love to one another and to all,** just as we do to you, so that He

may establish your hearts blameless in holiness before our God and Father at the coming of our Lord Jesus Christ with all His saints" (1 Thess. 3:12-13).

"But concerning brotherly love you have no need that I should write to you, for you yourselves are **taught by God to love one another**" (1 Thess. 4:9).

In 1 Corinthians 13 we are told that without love every spiritual gift is useless. I have known people who had major talent and ability, but they did not possess a deep love for people, so their talent was wasted. They have been unable to reach their potential. Individuals who are living the life of Radical Faith will be so much more than visionaries, healers, or great leaders. They will be persons primarily driven by their passionate love for Christ and their passionate love for people. Any other motivation will prevent them from paying the price required to fully obey God and live by faith.

Love is costly. Being engaged in others' lives can be draining. I know that at times throughout my journey of faith I have grown weary. When the financial load has been heavy or some other burden was weighing upon me and I couldn't humanly see my way through, I have grown discouraged in the battle. During some of those times my office window overlooked one of our school playgrounds. I would often step to the window and see those boys and girls swinging and playing cops and robbers and whatever else they were doing. Watching them, my heart would be lifted. Sometimes when I was discouraged I would walk through the halls of the school and look into the faces of the students. Something inside of me would well up and say, "I will fight on for these precious kids." At other times, I would be struggling through the battle and someone would walk into my office. He or she would tell me how in some way our ministry had helped to draw them to Jesus and change their life. I would be reminded once again why I had chosen this path of Radical Faith. The life of love is demanding. But once it becomes who you are, you cannot imagine living any other way, no matter the cost.

What Love Can Do

One Sunday morning, a Christian man who owned a carpet cleaning business showed up at our church in Virginia. He brought with him a tall, balding man in his 40s. I preached and then opened the altar for those who wanted to pray. The businessman and his guest both came to the altar. I soon learned that the man who owned the carpet business had been sharing his faith for some time with James Broughman (the tall, balding man). That morning James prayed and asked Christ to come into his life. As they left, the businessman said to me, "I live a good distance from here, and so I've done my part; the rest is up to you."

Within a few weeks we learned a lot more about James. He struggled greatly with depression, and he had no family who kept in contact with him. Outside of the lady who owned the restaurant where he worked, he did not have any true friends. We also learned that James could not read or write. He lived in a quiet lonely world by himself.

God helped our congregation to love James unconditionally. He did not have a car, so our people gave him rides all over town. He would often struggle to figure out why his phone was shut off or why his doctor changed his medicine, so our people helped him solve these problems. At some point, we invited James to hang out at the church during weekdays and do what he could to help. He was thrilled. Before long James became a major part of our ministry team. We learned that he was a phenomenal chef. He has cooked for our family retreats, men's retreats, summer camp meetings, and a thousand other smaller events. He loves serving in this way. We also learned that James loved to clean, so he became our staff janitor. Anytime I or another staff member would see something out of place in the church, we would simply mention it to James, and he would take care of it—with a smile. He loved it when I and other pastors would call on him.

James has now been a key member of the team at Parkway House of Prayer for many years. He is on disability and some days he has to take things slowly, but he has found his niche in the Body of Christ because people loved a man on whom family and society had given up.

The Love That Truly Loves

Authentic Christ-like love issues from a genuine love for Christ Himself. Do you want to love others as you should? Then love Christ first and foremost—love Him supremely. A selfless love for others will follow. No other approach, no other motivation will produce this kind of love. Unconditional, other-centered, servant love begins with a love for Christ.

Are you primarily motivated to serve out of a sense of duty or moral responsibility? Then when your sense of obligation wanes, so will the love you have manufactured.

Are you primarily motivated because you don't want to go to hell, or you want to store up some rewards in heaven? Then when your fear of hell or your reward seeking becomes inadequate, too distant to urge you on, your "love" will falter and fail.

Are you primarily motivated because you want others to think highly of you, or you want to be seen as a good person or a spiritual person? Then when you find easier ways or more self-beneficial ways to accomplish the same ends, your self-centeredness will reveal itself and your alleged love will be seen for what it has always been.

Let your *love* for Him and His love for you overflow into the lives of others.

Are you primarily motivated because you love the power or position love can bring? Then when you have the power or position you want, your so-called love will show itself as the selfish mask it always was.

Put Christ first instead.

Love Christ above all else.

Love Him with all you are and all you have.

Let your love for Him and His love for you overflow into the lives of others, be they in the Body of Christ or outside of it.

Then—and only then—will your love be selfless, sacrificial, unconditional, and unquenchable. His love will be your love. And His love endures and bears everlasting fruit.

This life of Radical Faith cannot be lived without a deep and intimate love relationship with Christ. Anything less will cause us to give up when the going gets tough.

Section 4

A Life of Supernatural Success

Chapter 23

What Is Supernatural Success?

I am an American. I have grown up in perhaps the most success-driven culture in the history of the world. In America we like to have everything bigger and better than everyone else, and in many ways we have succeeded in this effort. We have a very high standard of living, and upward social mobility is woven deeply into our psyche. I can never remember a day in my lifetime when I didn't believe that we had the most powerful military on earth. When it comes time for the Olympics, we usually win the most gold, silver, and bronze medals. Our national anthem, the "Star Spangled Banner," is played over and over again as our premier athletes win one medal after another. In America, bigger is almost always better. Our fast-food portions are huge as we have learned to upsize everything, including our waistlines. Success is a part of who we are. We reward successful people with money, fame, and honor. We now reward even immoral, successful people. As long as someone has achieved at a high level, we place them on a pedestal for all to admire.

Success is surely not bad in and of itself, and part of our success mentality comes from our Judeo-Christian heritage that teaches if you do the right things, God's natural and supernatural blessings will fall upon you. However, Satan loves to counterfeit every good thing, and he has done so with success. In the church world in America, we have adopted the unbiblical, American model of success. There is a brand of Christianity that I believe has become a hybrid mix of Christian teaching and materialism. Just start flipping through TV channels, and you will quickly find a preacher delivering this gospel of success. These preachers usually have large crowds hanging on their every positive word as they dream about how God is getting ready to bless them in a material way. I certainly believe that God blesses in a thousand ways those who honor Him with their lives and actions. Living in harmony with God's law will bring blessing. On the other hand, I also believe that we have cheapened the gospel and God Himself by turning Christianity into something that is unbiblical and even anti-biblical.

So what do I mean by supernatural success, and what does that have to do with the life of Radical Faith? Let's start with the success side of this discussion. Simply put, *supernatural success is the work of God that no human being can produce.* We can produce large crowds, magnificent facilities, phenomenal music and atmosphere, but only God can bring supernatural success. God may use and even help bring about large crowds, beautiful buildings, and the like, and when He is in such works, they are a part of the success only He can bring about. Notice, though, I said they are a part of His success, His work. But His work always exceeds the material, the physical, the financial. Human beings can use their intelligence, their know-how, their talents to move crowds, build organizations, and motivate people to give lots of money. But these happenings do not mean that God is in them, that He is aiding in their production. We as Christians need to be more discerning than that.

Here's what I have discovered. When we have enough faith to fully obey God and follow His plan, He makes things happen that we could never make happen by our own strength and ability. And God's success may often not be recognized for what it is and may even appear as failure before it is fully mature. Here's an example of what I mean.

> **God's success may often not be recognized for what it is and may even appear as failure before it is fully mature.**

When Earthly Failure Brings Heavenly Success

My father told me the story of an old-time evangelist who came to one of the many churches he attended as a boy. This preacher was called, not because he was the desired evangelist, but rather because the congregation couldn't agree on whom to call. The disagreement was fierce. Dad remembers one man standing up and saying something about his father starting this church and yet he had never been allowed to choose the evangelist. This man was offended and hurt over this matter. Church members eventually agreed to let a third party outside of the church choose who should come to preach this revival. Oh, does God have a way of getting His work done! The third-party chose.

On schedule, this bone-scraping evangelist showed up and began preaching. He preached it straight as a gun barrel and called the church to repentance. All day he would lay behind the pulpit in prayer. One night he told the congregation that God had revealed to him that there was a baby in the church. He flipped over a chair as if it was a stroller and headed down the center aisle. He stopped right where the man was sitting who had been complaining about not choosing the evangelist and said, "This is the baby in the church." The congregation was furious. They never invited this preacher back to their church. And according to everything one could see, this revival was a total failure.

> **We must get away from judging our work for the Lord from just an earthly point of view.**

However, this was where supernatural success came in. As a result of this preacher's influence, my dad was saved, and his two sisters began attending a Bible college. A year or so later, the sisters talked my dad into attending the same Bible college. This college and the connections he made as a result of his attendance there forever changed my dad's life. It was there he met my mother and began to be established in his walk with God. It was there he began to receive his passion for preaching and reaching needy souls. It was this school and its influence that helped my dad become a godly father who has produced children and grandchildren who are now taking the gospel around the world. From earth's point of view, the preacher Rev. Wilton Beck failed in his revival. However, perhaps as a result of lying behind the pulpit all day in prayer, from heaven's point of view, God blessed this revival with supernatural success that continues to this day. You can truthfully say that thousands have now been saved as a result of this one revival.

We must get away from judging our work for the Lord from just an earthly point of view. When we obey God, as Rev. Beck did, supernatural things happen!

By the way, forty plus years later, Wilton Beck's son Paul served as the minister of music at the church in Virginia where I was senior pastor. Wilton's legacy—and God's success—is still coming through his family.

The Flesh Versus the Spirit

Operating in the flesh is so much easier in some ways than operating in the Spirit. I wonder what would happen to most of our churches if we lost electricity for an extended period of time. Could we even worship? What if we didn't have the ability to dim the lights and show our videos on the screens? What if we couldn't use a microphone to project our voices or create the desired effect with the instruments? Would we still have the large crowds filing in if we didn't have air conditioning and state-of-the-art nurseries and restrooms?

We have learned how to produce desired results in attendance and atmosphere. Our people leave saying, "Wow! That was awesome this morning." But I often wonder how much supernatural work was really done. We spend most of our time getting the program, and even the sermon, just right. But how much time do we spend on our face before God asking Him for supernatural success in our services?

One of the reasons so little supernatural work is done in our lives and churches is because we have grown content with what the flesh can produce. The flesh can create great programs. The flesh can pay the budget. The flesh can hire competent and charismatic leaders. But the flesh cannot transform hearts and lives. The flesh cannot renew cities, states, and countries. Only a supernatural work of God can produce genuine revival and spiritual awakening, personally and corporately.

What could happen if many more Christians began to sell out to full obedience to Christ no matter the cost and no matter what it looked like to those who walk in the flesh?

What if more preachers preached what God wanted them to, even if it meant they got voted out or were never invited to return?

What if Christian workers spent more time in prayer than they did working on their power-point presentations?

We like to look at men and women who have left a great spiritual legacy and wish that we had whatever it was that made them so successful. Well, we do have what they had. We have the same God, the same Christ, the same Spirit, the same gospel. We are members of the same universal Body of Christ. And what else they had, we can also have. They had a heart that was willing to trust God against all odds and follow Him no matter where He led them. They had Radical Faith. We can have that too. Most of these men and women were more common than you would care to know, and yet their simple childlike faith led them to obey God and thus see supernatural results.

Do you want God to produce supernatural success in and through your life? If yes, all you must do is give Him all you are and have, to place everything before His throne, to surrender all to Him. Give Him your all. In return, He will give you His all. His all is infinite and eternal and unfailing. You will never receive anything from the world that even comes close to that gift and measure of success.

Chapter 24

Jesus' Faith Expectation

Jesus, God the Son in human flesh, obviously lived a life completely surrendered to God the Father's will. In other words, Jesus lived a life of Radical Faith. He followed the Father's plan all the way to the point of death. His commitment in the Garden of Gethsemane, "Not my will but yours be done," is the pattern for us to follow. However, more than just focusing on what He personally did, I want to briefly focus on what He instructed others to do as it relates to this matter of faith and how He responded to the faith of others.

Everywhere Jesus went He was looking to see if people really had faith in His ability to help them. His level of supernatural involvement was almost always influenced by an individual's level of faith. Notice what He said as He worked His way through His three years of ministry on earth.

- Then behold, they brought to Him a paralytic lying on a bed. When Jesus saw their **faith**, He said to the paralytic, "Son, be of good cheer; your sins are forgiven you." … then He said to the paralytic, "Arise, take up your bed and go to your house." And he arose and departed to his house (Matt. 9:2, 6-7, emphasis added).

- But Jesus turned around, and when He saw her He said, "Be of good cheer, daughter; your **faith** has made you well." And the woman was made well from that hour (v. 22, emphasis added).

- Then He touched their eyes saying, "Do you believe that I am able to do this?" They said to him, "Yes, Lord." Then He touched their eyes, saying, "According to your **faith** let it be to you." And their eyes were opened (vv. 28-30, emphasis added).

- And Jesus rebuked the demon, and it came out from him; and the child was cured from that very hour. Then the disciples came to Jesus privately and said, "Why could we not cast it out?" So Jesus said to them, "Because of your **unbelief**; for assuredly I say to you, if you have **faith** as a mustard seed, you will say to this mountain, 'Move from here to there,' and it will move; nothing will be impossible for you" (17:18-20, emphasis added).

- So they [his hometown crowd] were offended at Him. But Jesus said to them, "A prophet is not without honor except in his own country and in his own house." Now He did not do many mighty works there **because of their unbelief**" (13:57-58, emphasis added).

Jesus responded to people's faith. If they trusted Him, He gave them what they sought from Him—as long, of course, as it was good for them. If they distrusted Him or found Him offensive, they received little to nothing from Him. It is not that we can limit God by our faith, but that God usually chooses to limit Himself to our faith. He can and sometimes does "many mighty works" despite our disbelief (Matt. 13:58). But He does much more when we put ourselves in

> **Supernatural success is largely dependent upon our willingness to believe in who God is, in what He has said, and in what He can do in our lives, combined with our willingness to obey Him as a result of our belief.**

His hands and trust Him. Put another way, supernatural success is largely dependent upon our willingness to believe in who God is, in what He has said, and in what He can do in our lives, combined with our willingness to obey Him as a result of our belief.

The biblical record makes it clear that we see so little of God's supernatural work in our midst because He finds so little faith in our hearts. Instead we rely on ourselves—our own talents, experience, knowledge, relationships, and the like—far more than we rely on the all-powerful, all-knowing God. Why do we do this? Why do we so often seek God's help only as our action of last resort? What will it take for us to learn to go to Him first? Even the Son of God in His humanity surrendered His will to the Father's (John 5:30; 6:38). If He did so, how much more should we? And how much more would God do in and through us if we would trust Him first, foremost, and always—if we would seek to do His will instead of our own?

Do you want supernatural success? Then give yourself to the only One who can bring about that success. Nothing short of that will do.

Chapter 25

Slaying Giants

The entire doctrine of supernatural success comes to us from the divine revelation we have been given in the Holy Scriptures. Over and over again, God has interrupted history and the natural laws we live by to accomplish His purpose and plan. Most Christians do not have a problem with the supernatural God of the Bible, but when it comes to Him acting supernaturally today, that's another story. Why would we think that the God of all might and power would stop using His power in our day and age? The good news is, He hasn't, and He longs to make His glory and power known to us today.

Throughout this book, I have talked about biblical characters who exemplify what I am saying about the Christian life of

Radical Faith. I have done this because I believe the Bible is a living book written by a living God. I believe that when we work our way through the biblical accounts of God's supernatural work, they become real to us in a fresh way. I hold a very high view of Scripture. I believe it is divinely inspired and that God's grace flows through it anew in every word as we study it over and over again. Because of this, I want to highlight a few more accounts of God's supernatural activity in biblical history. Every time I read these accounts, my faith is strengthened.

David and Goliath

Most of us who were raised in a Christian church have heard the details of this story since our earliest days in Sunday school. If you are unfamiliar with this story, please read it in 1 Samuel 17 before you continue. In what follows, I assume you know the details of this biblical account.

There were so many reasons why David should not have fought Goliath and been picked as the new king over Israel.

- He was not a soldier, just a shepherd boy.
- He had no formal training to fight giants or be a king.
- He was small in stature. He was the last one picked among Jesse's sons when the prophet and priest Samuel was looking for the man God had chosen to replace King Saul.
- He was way too young to be fighting giants and leading a nation.

And yet, God chose David to face down the Philistine warrior

Goliath and become the next king of Israel.

Before we do a mighty work for God, I think that most of us experience fear. This has certainly happened to me every time God has asked me to step out in Radical Faith. However, there comes a point in time when God's Spirit overwhelms that sense of fear, and we march forward with unbelievable confidence. I have to believe that at the first sight of the nine-foot giant Goliath, David's heart felt a twinge of fear. At some point, though, the Holy Spirit emboldened David. Perhaps this happened when David looked around and saw all the Israelite soldiers shaking in fear. Maybe it was the first time he heard Goliath mock the name of the God of Israel. I don't know when his confidence in God soared, but I know that it happened

> **There comes a point in time when God's Spirit overwhelms our sense of fear and we march forward with unbelievable confidence.**

because of what we read in 1 Samuel 17:26: "Then David spoke to the men who stood by him, saying, 'What shall be done for the man who kills this Philistine and takes away the reproach from Israel? For who is this uncircumcised Philistine, that he should defy the armies of the Living God?'"

David then had to endure the faithless King Saul who told him that he could not kill Goliath. Then when David refused to back down, Saul continued to operate in the flesh by placing his armor on David. That didn't work. David could hardly walk in Saul's armor. Finally, Saul and the rest of the cowards in the Israelite army just accepted the fact that David was going to die at the hand of Goliath. They gave up, but God didn't! Listen to David, under the anointing of the Holy Spirit:

> And the Philistine said to David, "Come to me and I will give your flesh to the birds of the air and the beast of the field!" Then David said to the Philistine, "You come to me with a sword, with a spear, and with a javelin. But I come to you in the name of the Lord of hosts, the God of the armies of Israel, whom you have defied. This day the Lord will deliver you into my hand, and I will strike you and take your head from you. And this day I will give the carcasses of the camp of the Philistines to the birds of the air and the wild beasts of the earth, that all the earth may know that there is a God in Israel. Then all this assembly shall know that the Lord does not save with sword and spear; for the battle is the Lord's and He will give it into our hands" (1 Sam. 17:47).

David then actually ran towards Goliath and nailed him with a stone. The mighty Goliath fell down dead, utterly defeated by God's young shepherd boy.

Today's enemies of our God need to be reminded who they are fighting against. They are not fighting the anemic, scared, hunkered down Christian soldiers we find in most churches today. They are fighting the Lord of hosts and the King of kings. It's about time we show the world whom we really serve. *When God finds a man or woman who will trust in Him with all their heart, the church and the world are put on notice once again that God is still God Almighty!*

Without David's Radical Faith in God, this supernatural act of God would never have happened. Think of the consequences if David had not been a man of Radical Faith. No doubt the Philistines would have destroyed the Israelites. How many spiritual and physical battles have been lost in our lives and in the life of the church because there wasn't even one man or woman who believed God enough to fight the giant? David was willing to pay the ultimate price. If God wasn't in this one, he was a dead man. But David believed God; he put his trust in the One who is supremely trustworthy. Consequently, David was willing to go against the advice of every other Israelite who believed David would not return alive. David knew beyond a shadow of a doubt that God had the power to defeat Goliath, and he believed with all his heart he was the man God had called to get the job done. Oh that God would give us a lot more people with this confidence in God and His mission for their lives.

> David *believed* God; he put his trust in the One who is supremely trustworthy.

People have often asked me, since I started Renewanation in 2008 in the midst of the worst recession since the Great Depression, "Why did you start this new ministry in the midst of a recession?" I answer them like this. First of all, God told me to and that was good enough for me. Second, the last time I checked, God is never in a recession! Why do we always want to put God in our box? He is not limited by our limitations. Jesus asked the question, "When I return, will I find faith on the earth?" (Luke 18:8). When I look at the American church today, I can surely understand how relevant Jesus' question still is.

David had great faith in an even greater God. And that gave David the hope he needed to go against a mighty and dreaded enemy. Faith and hope go together. I have seen this in Scripture as well as in my own life and ministry. I appreciate the fact that over and over again, I have heard from seasoned saints and even the unsaved that although my preaching style is straightforward and challenging, it is also "hopeful and positive." There is one reason why it is this way. I believe with all my heart that we serve an awesome and mighty God who still longs to be involved in the affairs of mankind. I also believe that He is in the redeeming business. When I preach that adultery is sin, I also preach that God has the power and the desire to deliver us from our adulterous ways. When I preach that drunkenness is sin, I immediately follow with God's power to help overcome alcoholism. I really do believe that God can do anything, and that gives me a tremendous sense of hope in this darkened, sinful world we live in.

Our enemies may not be giant Philistine warriors, but they still have the power to slay us—unless we step out against them with our faith firmly planted in God. He will go before us, and in His power we can even defeat the enemies that lie within us. Imagine— we can have supernatural success within and without! We just need the right God—the one and only God revealed in Scripture—and the faith in Him to live life His way.

Is this what you really want?

Chapter 26

Doing It God's Way

The Bible is full of stories of God's supernatural work in the lives of men and women. One could write volumes just on God's supernatural activity. I have mentioned earlier the surrender and sacrifice of Noah, Abraham, Joseph, Moses, and others. They surrendered, suffered, served, and saw supernatural moves of God. I want to highlight one more Old Testament story before taking a brief look at the New Testament and then moving to a few of God's works I have seen in our day and time.

Faithful Youth and a Pagan King

Daniel. Shadrach. Meshach. Abednego. Four friends. Four young men. All captured Israelites. All sold out to God. No matter what circumstances they faced, they never stopped doing what they knew God wanted them to do.

Not long after the Babylonians took these men into captivity, they were forced to choose God's way or man's way when it came to the food they would eat. They chose God's way at great risk to themselves. In the process, they proved that His way was better than man's. God took notice of their radical trust in Him and blessed them. They ended up promoted into positions of significant leadership in the nation that had enslaved them (Dan. 1:1-21).

Sometime later, Daniel's three friends faced a more severe challenge—one that pitted them against king Nebuchadnezzar, the ruler of the Babylonian people. This king decided to authorize the construction of a great statue of himself and then demand that everyone in his kingdom worship it. I can't tell the story better than the Bible, so here is the account from Daniel 3:1-30.

The Image of Gold

Nebuchadnezzar the king made an image of gold, whose height was sixty cubits and its width six cubits. He set it up in the plain of Dura, in the province of Babylon. And King Nebuchadnezzar sent word to gather together the satraps, the administrators, the governors, the counselors, the treasurers, the judges, the magistrates, and all the officials of the provinces, to come to the dedication of the image which King Nebuchadnezzar had set up. So the satraps, the administrators, the governors, the counselors, the treasurers, the judges, the magistrates, and all the officials of the provinces gathered together for the dedication of the image that King Nebuchadnezzar had set up; and they stood before the image that Nebuchadnezzar had set up. Then a herald cried aloud: "To you it is commanded, O peoples, nations, and languages, that at the time you hear the sound of the horn, flute, harp, lyre, and psaltery, in symphony with all kinds of music, you shall fall down and worship the gold image that King Nebuchadnezzar has set up; and whoever does not fall down and worship shall be cast immediately into the midst of a burning fiery furnace."

So at that time, when all the people heard the sound of the horn, flute, harp, and lyre, in symphony with all kinds of music, all the people, nations, and languages fell down and worshiped the gold image which King Nebuchadnezzar had set up.

Daniel's Friends Disobey the King

Therefore at that time certain Chaldeans came forward and accused the Jews. They spoke and said to King Nebuchadnezzar, "O king, live forever! You, O king, have made a decree that everyone who hears the sound of the horn, flute, harp, lyre, and psaltery, in symphony with all kinds of music, shall fall down and worship the gold image; and whoever does not fall down and worship shall be cast into the midst of a burning fiery furnace. There are certain Jews whom you have set over the affairs of the province of Babylon: Shadrach, Meshach, and Abed-Nego; these men, O king, have not paid due regard to you. They do not serve your gods or worship the gold image which you have set up."

Then Nebuchadnezzar, in rage and fury, gave the command to bring Shadrach, Meshach, and Abed-Nego. So they brought these men before the king. Nebuchadnezzar spoke, saying to them, "Is it true, Shadrach, Meshach, and Abed-Nego, that you do not serve my gods or worship the gold image which I have set up? Now if you are ready at the time you hear the sound of the horn, flute, harp, lyre, and psaltery, in symphony with all kinds of music, and you fall down and worship the image which I have made, good! But if you do not worship, you shall be cast immediately into the midst of a burning fiery furnace. And who is the god who will deliver you from my hands?"

Shadrach, Meshach, and Abed-Nego answered and said to the king, "O Nebuchadnezzar, we have no need to answer you in this matter. If that is the case, our God whom we serve is able to deliver us from the burning fiery furnace, and He will deliver us from your hand, O king. But if not, let it be known to you, O king, that we do not serve your gods, nor will we worship the gold image which you have set up."

Saved in Fiery Trial

Then Nebuchadnezzar was full of fury, and the expression on his face changed toward Shadrach, Meshach, and Abed-Nego. He spoke and commanded that they heat the furnace seven times more than it was usually heated. And he commanded certain mighty men of valor who were in his army to bind Shadrach, Meshach, and Abed-Nego, and cast them into the burning fiery furnace. Then these men were bound in their coats, their trousers, their turbans, and their other garments, and were cast into the midst of the burning fiery furnace. Therefore, because the king's command was urgent, and the furnace exceedingly hot, the flame of the fire killed those men who took up Shadrach, Meshach, and Abed-Nego. And these three men, Shadrach, Meshach, and Abed-Nego, fell down bound into the midst of the burning fiery furnace.

Then King Nebuchadnezzar was astonished; and he rose in haste and spoke, saying to his counselors, "Did we not cast three men bound into the midst of the fire?"

They answered and said to the king, "True, O king."

"Look!" he answered, "I see four men loose, walking in the midst of the fire; and they are not hurt, and the form of the fourth is like the Son of God."

Nebuchadnezzar Praises God

Then Nebuchadnezzar went near the mouth of the burning fiery furnace and spoke, saying, "Shadrach, Meshach, and Abed-Nego, servants of the Most High God, come out, and come here." Then Shadrach, Meshach, and Abed-Nego came from the midst of the fire. And the satraps, administrators, governors, and the king's counselors gathered together, and they saw these men on whose bodies the fire had no power; the hair of their head was not singed nor were their garments affected, and the smell of fire was not on them.

Nebuchadnezzar spoke, saying, "Blessed be the God of Shadrach, Meshach, and Abed-Nego, who sent His Angel and delivered His servants who trusted in Him, and they have frustrated the king's word, and yielded their bodies, that they should not serve nor worship any god except their own God! Therefore I make a decree that any people, nation, or language which speaks anything amiss against the God of Shadrach, Meshach, and Abed-Nego shall be cut in pieces, and their houses shall be made an ash heap; because there is no other God who can deliver like this."

Then the king promoted Shadrach, Meshach, and Abed-Nego in the province of Babylon.

What an amazing account of Radical Faith in God! Oh that God would fill our hearts with this kind of bold, life-changing faith. These men counted their lives as nothing. They only had one desire and that was to serve the Lord God of heaven with faithful and true hearts. Their resolve is best seen in verses 16-18 when Nebuchadnezzar tries to give them a way out of the mess they had created. I can just hear what advice many Christians today would have given these three young men: "Now listen, we all know that we don't agree with bowing down to idols, but sometimes you just have to do what you have to do in order to make it through a situation without losing your job and, for goodness sakes, your lives."

Recently a public school basketball coach approached me and told me what had just happened to him. He said that during the halftime of a game he was coaching, he asked his team to bow their heads for a moment of silence. He did not pray, but some took it that he was asking his players to pray. One of the students complained, and this coach found himself in the principal's office. The principal looked at him and said something like this: "Coach, I know you are a Christian, and I am a Christian. However, when I walk through those doors I leave my Christianity behind because it is not allowed in this school, and you must do the same." What a shame.

I know that the public schools have banned every explicit notion of God and Christianity from their halls, but they did so because too many Christians bowed down in the years gone by rather than risking their jobs. Thankfully, there is still a remnant of teachers and administrators who are doing their best not to bow down in an environment that gets tougher on Christians every year. How many Christians bow down at work when asked to fudge the truth just a little bit? How many Christians, in order to make one more almighty dollar, make a sales pitch they don't really believe in? How many Christian men or women participate in questionable activities on business trips because they're afraid they won't get their next promotion if they look too holy? May God help us!

These young men in Daniel 3 refused to disobey God even if it meant they would be thrown into a fiery furnace. When standing before the king they spoke with a confidence and boldness that only God could have given them. Learn this: *When we step out on Radical Faith, the Holy Spirit of God empowers us to march forward.* I am learning this more and more every day on this journey of faith. I am amazed at how many people have asked me if I think Renewanation will make it or if I am doing okay as we face the challenge of building this ministry from the ground up. It often seems like they're asking me if I will quit if we don't hit the payload pretty soon. I deeply appreciate people's concerns, but in reality those are the wrong questions. The only question in my heart is, "Will I be faithful to God no matter what happens and no matter what it costs me?" I am not the one who determines the outcome. I am not the one who chooses my final lot in life. I may never see the full fruit of this ministry, or I may see major fruit. I surrender that to God daily. My only obligation is to give my best to the Master every single moment of every single day. If I experience material blessings on the journey, great; if not, it's still great as long as I remain true to God.

> When we step out on Radical Faith, the Holy Spirit of God *empowers* us to march forward.

Often we do not allow ourselves to get into a position where it's God or else. These young Israelite men knew that they would either experience God's supernatural help or their journey in this life was over. Either way, they were committed to serving Him. When we refuse to follow God into the unknown where His supernatural help is our only hope, we miss out on the opportunity to see Him work in a powerful way, and the world loses the opportunity to know who God really is and what He can do.

There was no way that Nebuchadnezzar was going to bow to the God of heaven if Shadrach, Meshach, and Abednego bowed their knees to the earthly king's idol. But once they walked all the way into the fiery furnace and God showed up, Nebuchadnezzar was nothing more than putty in theirs and God's hands. He actually began to praise the God of heaven and promoted these young men.

Our radical obedience and faith cause the world to see the glory and power of God. On the day that these young men walked through this frightening situation, they had no idea that billions of people would someday read every detail of their story. *That was something only a supernatural God could make happen, and He did!* Thousands of years after they exercised Radical Faith, you and I today are once again being challenged to do the same as a result of their actions. We often like to think that our lives really aren't all that important and that no one is really watching. But our lives are important, and God is watching our every move. One day He may just choose to tell the whole world how we trusted Him.

If we want to experience supernatural success, we must surrender our all to God. We must be willing to sacrifice and suffer if that is what following God requires, and we must be primarily motivated by a passionate love for Christ and people.

Chapter 27

God's Kingdom Advances

The New Testament is packed with stories detailing the supernatural success that Radical Faith and obedience produce (see the Gospels and Acts).

This historical record starts with the virgin Mary as she hears from the angel and believes she will become pregnant with the long-awaited Messiah. Joseph, her husband-to-be, is then asked to trust God with her miraculous pregnancy. Their son, Jesus, comes along and lives His fully human life in total dependence upon the Father's instruction and the Holy Spirit's guidance and empowering work. Once Jesus starts His ministry, He does everything backwards according to the Jews. They were looking for a King who would build a great following and army so that they could overthrow

Roman rule. Jesus instead obscurely wanders around choosing twelve men to spend most of His time with. From the outside, this in no way looked like the King of kings building His kingdom on earth. Finally, Jesus goes to the cross and dies. How anti-climactic! Then Jesus rises from the dead and begins appearing to eleven of His closest followers. Stunned yet now fully convinced of Jesus' divine-human identity and message, they wait as instructed with His other followers in an upper room in Jerusalem until they are filled with the Holy Spirit on the day of Pentecost. Once the Spirit comes and fills them with new power, these disciples burst onto the streets of Jerusalem proclaiming the good news about Jesus' resurrection and the salvation He brings. They are persecuted off and on for decades, and most of them are eventually killed as a result of their obedience to Christ.

Against all odds, Christianity continues to grow and thrive in a world that is growing more and more hostile towards it.

These faithful disciples were not the intellectuals or the great businessmen or the admired craftsmen of their day. But Jesus had fed them with spiritual food, trained them for ministry, modeled ministry for them, and given them the Great Enabler, the Holy Spirit, to empower them and guide them. Then to their number, the resurrected Jesus added an anti-Christian zealot, a hater and persecutor of the faith. This man named Paul, ended up writing most of the New Testament and successfully evangelizing and planting churches in various cities throughout much of the Roman Empire. Together these Christ-followers were used by God to spread Christianity all over the known world. The very existence of Christianity and its continued influence in the world today are perhaps the greatest evidences of the power of the life of Radical Faith. Against all odds, Christianity continues to grow and thrive in a world that is growing more and more hostile towards it.

The apostle Paul's life is a beautiful example of supernatural success produced by Radical Faith. He never had a great ministry organization, and he was often maligned and abused. He spent a lot of time getting run out of towns or locked up in some awful prisons. He was often broke, hungry, and homeless. Certain members of the church questioned his motives and disagreed on whether he was a servant being used by God. He died a gruesome death at the hands of Nero's soldiers. In our day, we would have called him a maverick preacher who never quite understood how to put it all together. If we were just studying history and did not know how God used Paul in the long run, we could have pointed out the immorality in his Corinthian church plant and said, "See, he didn't really know how to make disciples." We could have picked apart so much of his ministry. However, in God's eyes he was no doubt the greatest messenger of the gospel ever known to mankind. His Holy Spirit inspired writings have now been studied and read by more people than perhaps any other writings in the history of the world. They have transformed entire cultures and nations. *Now that is supernatural success that can only be attributed to a supernatural God!*

We have developed this very short timeline for success in our world today. We evaluate a person's life over a thirty-to-forty-year span of time and pronounce our judgment. God sees through a very different set of lenses. Our responsibility is not to guarantee our own success on a standard used by this world. Our responsibility is to live a life of Radical Faith and obedience and let God keep score.

When we do what God asks us to do, He multiplies our frail human efforts and amazing things happen. Oh what a freedom it is to live for the approval of God and God alone! Only then can we rest in the prospect that if we are fully obeying God, our labor will bear fruit—His fruit, which is everlasting and incorruptible.

> **Oh what a *freedom* it is to live for the approval of God and God alone!**

Chapter 28

Faith, Family, and Prodigals

The only true success I have experienced in working for God has come about as a result of Radical Faith. In the rest of this book, I will highlight a few of the accounts of supernatural success I have been privileged to witness.

I have already shared with you some of the ways God has worked in the lives of my family. I told you of the faith of my two grandmothers who saw just a little of the fruit that came from their lives of Radical Faith. Though they were bound most of their lives to very humble circumstances with husbands who were difficult to live with and often worked against their faith, their commitment to God bore incredible fruit. As I write today my two grandmothers have twenty-one children, grandchildren, and great-grandchildren who are preachers, married to preachers, or preparing to be preachers. Others from their family have served overseas in world missions or are in preparation to go, and many are singing the gospel around the globe. Still others are involved in Christian education, business, medicine, and many other professions. Only a supernatural God could take the humble and difficult lives of two country women and bless them like this. Neither one of my grandmothers spoke great English. They didn't dress fancy, and their houses were nothing to write home about. On the surface, even the people they attended church with didn't see them as all that special. And yet, their faithfulness to God has been supernaturally blessed beyond anything they could have hoped for, but not beyond anything they prayed for. My sister Becky recently told me that Grandma Keaton McKinney said before she died that her dream had been to become a missionary after her husband was killed in WWII. People told her there was no way she could fulfill this dream, so she gave up on it and raised her five kids. It was not lost on Grandma or Becky that somehow Grandma's call to mission's work was being fulfilled through Becky and my sister Sandy. God has a powerful way of rewarding faithful people! Both of my grandmothers enjoyed watching preachers on TV. No doubt they would have been greatly blessed to know that my sister Kim and her family sang on Charles Stanley's *In Touch* television program and are performing on many other nationally televised programs.

> If you will stay faithful to the Lord, you will reap a *spiritual* harvest beyond your wildest imaginations.

When we stay true to God in the midst of all of life's circumstances, supernatural success comes our way. If you're reading this and your life is difficult, don't you dare give in or give up because of Satan's lies. If you will stay faithful to the Lord, you will reap a spiritual harvest beyond your wildest imaginations. You may not see all your faith has produced on this side of heaven, but you will certainly see it on the other side. I have no doubt that the apostle Paul, for example, is thoroughly amazed at what God has done for the last two thousand years through his faithful ministry. And yet the church worldwide continues to benefit from Paul's ministry, especially from the writings of this great servant of God. This same God is at work in you. Don't shortchange what He can do through you. You don't have to be absolutely perfect. Except for Jesus, who in biblical history was? Who in church history was? No one. God is not looking for perfect people, just sold out people. He wants people who trust Him, who walk in faith, who follow Him no matter what. Through them He can accomplish the most. You can be such a person.

My Father and Mother

I want to return to my parents for a little while. I am not trying to elevate our family above our humble position in God's economy. I certainly make no claim that our family is above failures and struggles; on the contrary, there have been many. However, if telling our story will challenge one other person to sell out to God and let Him use them, no matter where they come from, then it's a story worth telling. Besides, this is a story I know firsthand.

I mentioned earlier about the circumstances of my parents'

lives. In many people's eyes my mother and father were improbable candidates for God's use. They faced difficulty, including abuse, as children. Even in Bible college some made the case that my father James Keaton was never going to amount to anything. However, as God gained control of their lives, they were empowered to make the choice to live the life of Radical Faith. As we were growing up, my father and mother were 100 percent sold out to Jesus and full-time ministry. They were not in the ministry because they had to be. They were in the ministry because it was the love of their hearts. My dad operated in five primary spheres of ministry. He loved the local church, evangelism (through revival and camp ministry), Christian education, world missions, and music. He pastored and grew several different churches. He has preached at over two hundred camp meetings and more revivals than we could possibly remember. He started a Christian school in 1976 and was the president of a Bible college for ten years. As we were growing up, our family sang wherever Dad preached. As a pastor and the president of a world missions organization, he led many people to get involved with him in worldwide missions. He also dreamed about planting churches in Virginia throughout his lifetime of ministry.

In many people's eyes my mother and father were improbable candidates for God's use.

Over the last decade, God has begun to take the passions and dreams He placed in Dad's heart to a totally new level. Seven of Dad's kids are either preachers or married to preachers. Between my brothers and sisters, we have so far pastored churches for a combined total of almost a hundred years. Several of us now preach or sing at camps and revivals. As I will tell about shortly, God has allowed my brother Troy and me to be involved in church planting in Virginia. My brother Troy now leads this planting effort that is going strong. One day as I was driving down the road with Dad, I said, "Dad, do you remember those dreams you always had to plant churches in Virginia?" "Yes," he replied. "Well," I added, "God is fulfilling that dream through your sons." He beamed with pride.

In 2002 God called me to start a Christian school in Roanoke, Virginia. As we were starting Parkway Christian Academy, I kept thinking about the school my dad had started when I was only in the third grade. I even adopted the school song my dad had written so many years earlier. The experience gave me a feeling of deja vu. Now, I am leading an effort to make weekday Christian education available to the masses across America and someday to the world. God is allowing me through the ministry of Renewanation to take Dad's dreams way beyond where he was able to take them.

My sisters Sandy and Becky, along with their families, have spent a combined twenty-one years in the Philippines and the Ukraine as full-time missionaries. Becky's husband Tim is now the director of World Missions for his denomination.

When it comes to music, we used to sing as a family. With nine kids we were quite the road show. Our mother and all of our five sisters play the piano quite well, but since we were little we had this amazing little piano player in our midst. Kimberly started playing at about four years old and never stopped. By the time she was seven she was our full-time church pianist. At eleven she was on the road playing for groups, and today she travels with her family "The Collingsworth Family." Her family recently won their first Dove Award and have been privileged to sing and record with the Gaithers on many occasions. God has allowed Kim and her family to take my father and mother's love of music ministry beyond anything they ever imagined.

I'm sharing all of this with you to celebrate in print what God has done in the small world of my family, and to give you just one more example of what God can do and wants to do in the lives of those who love Him. My father loves his Lord and Savior and his love shows through his obedience to God. My father's willingness to stay in tune with the Holy Spirit and his willingness to sacrifice and suffer in order to obey God's leadership are now producing a level of success that can only be attributed to the personal, supernatural, faithful, gracious God. My father now has forty-one grandchildren and six great-grandchildren. Many of these are already in ministry, and many more will no doubt go into full-time Christian ministry. Others of them are in the military or will be called into medicine, business, or law to be salt and light in our culture. Only God can possibly comprehend the full impact a few lives, completely sold out to Jesus, will have for time and eternity.

I am so thankful that my grandmothers and my parents lived the life of Radical Faith. Truly they have experienced the truth of Psalm 37:4. *Delight yourself also in the Lord, And He shall give you the desires of your heart.*

Love for a Prodigal

Faith, even in a family, does not guarantee the absence of faithlessness. We can all doubt, all struggle, all fail. And at times we can turn away from what we have been taught and witnessed firsthand. My family is no exception. We know about prodigals, waywards within.

I had a wayward brother, Brian. Things took place in his life that got him off track. He ended up wandering far from God. Brian's struggles broke all of our hearts, but my father's love for him never wavered, and he led the rest of our family to love Brian unconditionally during his dark days. During some of Brian's most precarious moments, my father wrote him a poem. To this day, it reminds me of my father's great love for his children. Even more, though, it illustrates God's love for all of His children. It's called "Daddy, do you love me?"

"Daddy, do you love me?"

Do you still love me, Daddy, after all I've said and done? Now I've broken all the fences, and from your love I've tried to run.

I've treated rules like they were nothing, mattered not from God or man. I've disregarded all your wishes, responded not to your loving hand.

Mother's love was not important, nor the tears she shed each night. I'd go on and do it my way, I'd show them all it will turn out right.

But, Dad, the sting of sin is awful, leaving scars I can't erase. How I wish I'd never started hastening age upon your face.

Tell me, Daddy, can you love me, after how I broke your heart? Is there hope awaiting, can I make another start?

Yes, my son, your dad still loves you, more than you will ever know. Praying prayers that always follow, wherever you may choose to go.

I do confess my heart is broken. My hopes for you had been so high. Wanting you to follow Jesus, knowing Satan is so sly.

I've held my breath as I've watched you wander, close to the edge of eternal despair, and turned to God, when you wouldn't listen, trusting Him to hear my prayer.

I ask you, son, do you remember, when you were but just a child? We went to see a barber on a winter day so mild.

You and your three fine brothers, planned to race on to the car, 'twas just across the boulevard, it wasn't very far.

Your brothers saw it coming, the car that sped so fast, but you, the youngest child, could only think of winning a race at last.

Into the path of sure destruction, you ran on without a thought, and son, there would have been a funeral, but in angel's arms you were caught.

Instead of death we saw mercy. Instead of three my sons are four. Yes, my boy, your daddy loves you, but the Savior loves you more.

But, Daddy, do you really love me? Some bad habits I've

acquired. And now it seems that I may never reach the heights you have aspired.

The chains of sin seem oh so binding. How I wish they'd let me go. If I could only start all over, I'd do it different, that I know.

I see the smoke curling upward, from the ashtray on the stand. Dad, how I wish I had listened. Tobacco never makes a man.

Daddy, I've lied, I've stolen and cheated. I've been immoral and I'm ashamed. But, Daddy, one more time I ask you, do you love me just the same?

Yes, my son, I really love you, and you must know that I always will, and your mother loves you dearly, brothers and sisters love you still.

But my child there is one who loves you, and He will gladly take your case. He will fight your battles for you, and back down devils face to face.

I've told you before, His name is Jesus. The chains of sin He will destroy. You see He's done the same for others, and He will for you my wayward boy.

But you must trust Him and believe Him. Turn away from your life of sin. For 'tis through the blood of Jesus, you can and will be whole again.

You ask me if I love you, son. Of that you can be sure. But please my child remember, the blessed Jesus loves you more.

As I pastored in Hollywood, I carried a heavy burden for Brian. I tried to help him, but my efforts seemed unsuccessful.

Unknown to me, a little Catholic girl named Kristin came from Missouri to visit her grandmother in Florida. I had led her grandmother and grandfather to Christ, along with scores of Kristin's aunts, uncles, and cousins. Grandma Bunk brought Kristin to one of our services. Kristin later told me that I scared her half to death because she had never heard a straightforward sermon about the need to repent and be saved. She then sought the Lord a few times, but never really seemed to cross the line of faith. I was later told that she could never get away from the truth she had heard proclaimed.

What *story* will God write through your family, if you will live the life of Radical Faith and be obedient to His leadership?

I lost touch with her until I heard that somehow she had met my youngest brother, and they were together. I was very concerned that my brother was not where he should be and that his involvement with Kristen might lead her to great disappointment. In spite of my concern, they were married while living in Kentucky.

Shortly after they were married, she led my brother to a little church in their town. Both of them surrendered their lives fully to Christ. Over the last fifteen years Kristen has been a rock in Brian's life. He has been deployed on a number of occasions in his service for the U.S. military. Today Kristin stands by his side as he struggles with his injuries from war. Kristin is teaching their children to love and serve Jesus. She is an amazing Christian, wife, and mother. I have often told her, "God sent me to save your family's lost souls, and you saved my lost brother." That is supernatural success!

What story will God write through your family, if you will live the life of Radical Faith and be obedient to His leadership? That story may differ greatly from mine in its details, but in its results it will show all the earmarks of the kind of success only God can bring.

Chapter 29

God in Hollywood

I have already shared some stories about my time as a pastor in Hollywood, Florida and Roanoke, Virginia. My move to Hollywood was especially trying. The church there had never paid a pastor in its history. This church was outside of the denomination I was primarily raised in; it was quite small, and it was in desperate need of new life. Even the city in which this church resided was very rough and needy. Why should I go to such a church when I had better opportunities closer to my home in Indiana? I wanted to stay where I was comfortable, in a place I knew. But God had other plans. He told me, "Go to Hollywood!" So I went—and it was no picnic. My finances were tough. My family and I lived in culture shock for two or three years. And Satan constantly tried to tell me that I was wasting my time. But God showed me that my time was His and that He would never waste it. I saw Him move and work wonders. And the supernatural results continue to this day. Here is yet one more story about His amazing work.

Ray and Terri

In 1993 I met a lady named Terri Campbell. This sweet lady was working her way through post-traumatic stress disorder as a result of very difficult childhood and teen experiences. She had also lost a six-year-old daughter to leukemia. When I first met Terri she was struggling to get out of her house and at times even her bedroom because of her overwhelming fear.

One Sunday morning Terri gave her life to Christ and began to walk the road of faith. God began a beautiful process of healing her heart, mind, and soul. Within a few months of her conversion, I began leading a new converts Bible study in her home with about twenty-four in attendance. It was exciting to work with these new Christians.

I don't recall when I first met Terri's husband Ray, but I know he wasn't friendly. I later found out that he thought Christians were a bunch of weirdoes, and he didn't want anything to do with them. I remember sitting with him in a hospital waiting room for several hours one day. I don't think he spoke more than ten words to me. I didn't get good vibes from him. Often when we met at his home for Bible study, he would come home from his job as the senior manager of a large department store. He usually walked in the door near the study's end. He would walk to the kitchen and from there just stare at us while we were preparing to leave. He gave me every impression that he was not fond of any of us.

On an August Sunday morning in 1995, Terri walked in the door of the church looking like she had just won the lotto. She was smiling and in a very secretive way pointing behind her. When I looked, I saw Ray walking behind her. He was dressed in his typical business suit. He came up to me and shook my hand. I couldn't believe it. I was so excited that he had chosen to attend church for the very first time. I knew that he had grown up in a mostly irreligious home and had almost no church background or understanding. Yet, here he was, n this small church, among people he had seemed to care nothing about. Well, as it turned out, Ray and Terri's children were being featured in our Vacation Bible School program that morning. This was why Ray was there. The service went great, and Terri left just knowing that this was the beginning of something new in Ray's life.

When they got home from church that day, Ray burst Terri's bubble of joy. He looked at her and said, "I went to church for one reason today and that was my kids. Don't expect me to ever go back." Late that night Terri called me, devastated.

A few weeks went by. Then one Sunday morning Ray was up early putting his suit on. His six-year-old daughter Jennifer bounced into his **"Daddy's going to church!"** bedroom and asked, "Daddy, are you getting ready for work?" He later told me that he was terribly embarrassed to admit to his young daughter that he was returning to church with her that morning. Jennifer exploded with joy and began running around the house proclaiming to everyone, "Daddy's going to church!" Ray came back to church that morning for reasons he could not explain. He didn't yet understand the convicting power of the Holy Spirit that was drawing him towards Christ.

From that Sunday on, for the next couple of months, Ray hardly missed a service. Finally, on October 8, 1995, I had a guest speaker. He preached a simple message, "What Do You Have If You Have Jesus?" One of his points was, "If you have Jesus you will have PEACE." Toward the end of the sermon I heard someone sobbing behind me. I had no thought that it was Ray Campbell.

If you have Jesus you will have *peace*.

But at the close of the sermon, the preacher stepped down front and asked a simple question: "Does anyone here want to invite Jesus into your life?" I heard shuffling feet, and to my great surprise a weeping Ray Campbell stumbled his way to the altar. I jumped up and knelt beside him. I asked him if he was ready to surrender his life to Christ. "Yes," he finally got out. I then asked him if he knew how to pray. "No," he said. So I led him through a simple sinner's prayer. Then instantaneously, Ray Campbell became a new creation in Christ Jesus. He stood up with a look I had never seen on his face. At that moment the Holy Spirit said to me, "He will pastor with you someday." I wasn't on cloud nine that day; I was on cloud nine hundred—and Ray's wife Terri was somewhere up above me.

We had spiritual emphasis week going on through Wednesday of the following week, and Ray was at every service. It is so refreshing to see people experience true conversion to Christ. When they do, they are hungry for God! I knew from day one that God had a unique path laid out for Ray and Terri.

Ray continued to grow by leaps and bounds over the next couple of months. One day I stopped by his house. For the first time since his conversion experience he looked troubled. He said, "You know I'm going to have to start working on Sundays again, don't you?" I had no idea where this was coming from. He had well over a hundred employees working for him, and he had been able to attend Sunday services every week since his conversion. To my knowledge we had never talked about him working on Sundays. I looked at him and said, "You just do what the Lord is telling you to do, and I will support you." He left as Terri and I talked for a few minutes about another Bible study she was involved in.

When I drove away from their house that day, I was troubled. I could tell that Ray was perhaps facing the first serious spiritual battle since he had been saved.

Late that night, I received a call from Terri. She said, "Pastor Jeff, you will not believe what happened tonight. Ray came home after several hours away and called me and the three kids to the table for a family meeting. He commenced to tell us that God had given him clear instructions today. He was to make worship on Sundays a very high priority, and he was not to work unless there was an emergency and no other managers were available. He said that God had also told him to start giving 10 percent of his income to the church. He went on to spell out what this would mean. First, he told us that he would most likely lose his job. This would mean that the kids would no longer get the best toys, vacations, etc. At the end of the meeting he asked for everyone's vote on his decision." Terri said it was unanimous in favor of Dad attending church every

Sunday, even if it meant they didn't have all the money they were used to.

Ray approached me at church the next day and told me about what he "thought" God was saying to him. I realized something big was going on here. I had never had a new Christian come to this depth of surrender so fast. I told Ray to do what God was telling him to do, and I would be there to support him every step of the way.

The next day Ray went to work and contacted his district manager. He told him that he planned on attending church every Sunday instead of being at work. He assured the DM that he would make sure every Sunday was covered and that he would be there if other managers were unavailable. He also told the DM that he had committed to working every Saturday so other managers could have a break on the weekend as well. The district manager said, "No problem. Your store is number one in sales in the entire region. Just keep it that way." Wow! That was easy. Ray called me and we both celebrated.

A few days later someone at a higher corporate level caught wind of this. This person contacted the district manager and said "No way" to Ray's decision. Company personnel contacted Ray and told him that his "request" would set a bad precedent, so they were going to deny it. Ray made it clear to them that this wasn't a request—it was a religious conviction. They ignored his plea and said, "You will either be here on Christmas Eve Sunday or you will turn in your keys the day after Christmas."

I will never forget that Christmas Eve Sunday. Ray came to church that morning bearing the cross that Christ was asking him to bear. He was not his usual happy self. He came back that night for our candlelight communion service. His countenance was heavy as he knew being there meant he would lose a job he had spent twenty years to earn. I watched him as the candle he was holding flickered on his face. My heart was heavy with his. I knew the enemy would love to use this experience to destroy Ray's newfound faith. I was worried as a pastor about him being able to handle the pressure of losing such a high-paying job. It all seemed so noble, but what if it didn't all work out? I have rarely seen God ask a new Christian to step out on Radical Faith so early in their walk with Him. I knew this meant God had something very special for Ray, but I just hoped he would make it through the process.

I knew the enemy would love to use this experience to destroy Ray's newfound faith.

On Tuesday, December 26, 1995, Ray was met in his office by the district manager and a representative from corporate headquarters. They slid a paper across his desk and said, "Sign your resignation, and give us your keys." Ray looked at them and said, "I am not resigning; you are firing me." He chose not to sign the paper, but he handed them the keys and said, "May God bless you." At no point in this process was Ray ever bitter or hateful toward those who fired him. Later on we learned that this company had already been successfully sued by another employee over this same issue. Ray had a Christian attorney who started the process pro bono, but Ray stopped him. He felt like God was asking him to walk away from everything he had once held dear.

As soon as Ray called me and gave me the details, I began to cry out to God. I was saying things like, "God, now you have to come through. He needs to see your power. He has sacrificed his twenty-year career for you." I was pretty sure God was going to show up quick and big time.

Ray began to look for another job. He was forty years old, and as he went from place to place, they thought he was either lying about what had happened at his former job or he had lost his mind. Companies could not believe that he had given up such a high paying job just because he felt like he should go to church on Sunday. Most of the smaller stores wouldn't hire him because he was overqualified, and they couldn't come close to matching his pay. They were all afraid they would spend the money to train him, and then another larger department store chain would offer him a much better paying job. One month passed, then two, three, four, five, six months. Still no job.

One day with tears welling up in his eyes, he looked at me and said, "I don't think you know what I'm going through. These people think I'm a man in my mid-life crisis who has gone off the deep end." I looked at him and assured him I didn't know exactly what he was going through, but that I was going to stand with him.

Over the course of those long six months, I told Ray that God had him in a spiritual incubator. He probably read about thirty books that I gave him, and he read the Bible like there would be no tomorrow. One day I stopped by his house, and he said he had finished the book of Revelation that day and had almost completed the book of Acts.

During this time when he could not find work, Ray was literally experiencing a "death to self" experience like few I had seen. I noticed one day that his high dollar gold chain was no longer on his arm. He later told me that he had purchased that as a status symbol when he received his last promotion. He stopped wearing it because he no longer needed such a symbol. One day I took him with me as I was preaching at a youth camp. We were walking across the campus, and I asked if he had a pen I could borrow. He handed me a beautiful pen that I later learned was a Mont Blanc. As I tried to give it back to him, he said, "No, you just keep it." I had no idea how much this pen had cost him. He later told me that it was just one more status symbol that he no longer needed as a Christian. He said he had purchased it because he signed documents all day, and he wanted people to know who he was. God was stripping away all that Ray had used to prop himself up through the years, so He could rebuild him in His image. During those months, he sold his '55 Chevy and cashed in his 401k. By June of 1996, there wasn't much left of the old Ray Campbell. He was now a man who had given up almost everything to follow Christ.

> **God was stripping away all that Ray had used to prop himself up through the years so He could rebuild him in His image.**

One day he walked into my office and said, "It is finished. I have surrendered the very last thing I was holding onto." I asked him what it was. He said, "Well, yesterday, as I was praying, God revealed to me that I had not surrendered my family to Him and His care." He said, "I have been telling God through all of this, 'If you don't give me a job, who is going to take care of my family?'" He then said, "Yesterday, I told God that even if he never gives me another job, I know He will take care of my family, so that issue is settled." He then said, "And there was one more thing. Ever since Terri and I lost Brandi to cancer at six years of age, I could never imagine losing another child. I've been telling God since I got saved, 'You can have everything, but you cannot ever take another one of my children.'" He continued, "Yesterday, I surrendered my three children to Jesus. If He wants to take them, I will trust that He knows best." I was blown away. A man who had only been saved for nine months had reached a level of absolute surrender that most Christians who have been saved for thirty years have not reached.

A man who had only been saved for nine months had reached a level of absolute surrender that most Christians who have been saved for thirty years have not reached.

Within a week or two after that, God gave Ray a new job. He found a furniture store that was closed on Sundays. God said, "Walk in there and tell them you're supposed to work here." This company had about sixty stores. Somehow, on this day, the owner of the entire chain was sitting in the manager's office. Ray walked in and said, "I am supposed to work here." When the owner saw Ray's credentials, he was almost embarrassed to tell Ray what he could offer. Ray said, "I don't care what you pay me. This is where the Lord has told me to work." Believe it or not, this made sense to the owner; you see, he was a Christian too. He created a new assistant manager's position and hired Ray on the spot. He started him out at a lowly $400 per week. Within a short time Ray was a store manager. Soon they opened a new store for Ray to manage. His pay kept climbing, but God had other plans.

Within a year of his conversion, Ray began to feel a call into pastoral ministry. He began in-depth studies with a retired pastor and loved every minute of the work. At some point the Lord said to me, "Send him away for more formal training." He already had two business degrees, but he chose to go to a Bible college and start from the ground up. It was so hard to send him and his family away after three and a half years in our church. They were heavily involved there. But I knew they had to leave, and I supported them in that decision.

The life of Radical Faith will produce supernatural success!

In God's providence, Ray ended up finding a small church to pastor while he was attending college. I will never forget the day I drove to Ohio for his graduation. We beamed with pride as Ray, at forty-seven-years old, graduated summa cum laude with a degree in pastoral ministries. He continued to pastor in Ohio until 2005 when he moved to Virginia to join our staff. God kept His word that he gave me the day Ray was saved. For my last six years at Parkway, Ray was right by my side and quickly became one of our top associate pastors. His wife Terri is a wonderful teacher in the Christian school we started. God is amazing!

When I was contemplating whether or not I should take the struggling little church in Hollywood, Florida, Ray and Terri

Campbell were lost in their sin. I didn't know their names or even that they existed. But as a result of our family's willingness to obey God against all advice and odds, we now celebrate the supernatural success in Ray and Terri's transformed lives. *The life of Radical Faith will produce supernatural success!*

Chapter 30

1000 - 100 - 10

M any churches are about three things: attendance, building, and cash—the ABCs of an allegedly successful ministry. Each of these have to do with numbers: how many people are coming to the service, and how can we increase the numbers; when can we build, how long will that take, and what will it cost; and how much money came in and how can we increase the amount given. These things are not bad in themselves, but when they become a church's focus, they subvert its mission, which is to bring people to Christ and mature them in the faith. Ministry should be about lives, not numbers—people, not possessions—conformity to Christ, not the cash on hand and how to get more of it. So in my ministry I have downplayed the numbers game. I have worked to keep first things first.

One day, however, God added to my perspective. He made three numbers a central focus of my ministry. Here's what happened.

Ministry by the Numbers

The Thursday before Mother's Day in 2000, I received a phone call from a pastor in Roanoke, Virginia. I knew Steve Parker since our dads were both camp meeting evangelists, but we were not well acquainted. Steve shared briefly with me about the church he had been pastoring for the last seven years. God had blessed, and they had grown from about 40 to 200 in attendance. He didn't tell me much more in our five-minute conversation because I wasn't interested in hearing more. He did say that God had called him to leave the church and wondered if I would be interested in becoming a candidate for pastor. I quickly told him "no thanks" and ended the call.

I was still living as if I would be in Hollywood the rest of my life. God had promised that if He ever wanted me to leave, He would make it so clear I could not miss it. In the days that followed Steve's call from Virginia, I was in total turmoil. All I could think about was Roanoke, Virginia. I knew I was in trouble when I went home on several occasions and found my wife researching all the details of Roanoke. She had never before shown any interest in moving.

About eight days into this experience, I said to God, "God, would you either get Roanoke, Virginia off my mind or make clear what you're trying to say to me?" By this time, I couldn't even focus on my duties in Hollywood.

God spoke to me and said, "Pick up that phone and call the pastor in Virginia."

I argued with God for a moment, "But God, I already told him I am not interested."

God said, "Call him back."

I went over, picked up the phone, and called Steve. I started by telling him, "I'm not saying I'm interested. I'm simply calling because God told me to."

Steve said, "I knew you would be calling me back." He later told me that as he was fasting from food for forty days, God had told him his time at Parkway was finished and that almost immediately God gave him my name to call.

To make a long story short, God called me to move to Roanoke, Virginia and made it so clear I couldn't do anything else and remain obedient. We said our tearful goodbyes to so many wonderful sons and daughters in the Lord in Hollywood and moved to Virginia in the fall of 2000. We were in culture shock for the first year as we tried to adjust to a more rural pastorate with a very different mentality than we had been used to. God began to move, and over the first two years we grew to more than 250 in Sunday morning attendance. Things were going well.

One August day in 2002, I was driving back from a few days on a lake with my brother Troy and his family. My family was asleep, and I was exhausted. As I drove along, the Lord began to speak into my heart. "Jeff, this is what I am doing at Parkway in this decade from 2000 to 2010. I am going to raise up 1,000 new disciples, call 100 people into full-time Christian ministry, and help you plant 10 new churches." This was big. For a church of such a moderate size as ours, these goals were out of reach—without divine help, that is. Then the Lord said, "Go home this weekend and share this with the congregation."

This is where my sensitivity against making numbers an important part of ministry raised its head. I didn't want to obey God on this. I wrestled with Him over it. I have never liked to throw numbers around. I have rarely even set an attendance goal for a special Sunday. But God was making Himself very clear. I knew that in order to be obedient to God, I would have to present this new vision to my congregation the following Sunday.

> **I didn't want to obey God on this. I wrestled with Him over it.**

On that fateful Sunday morning in August 2002, I said something like this: "I am a fallible human being, and I may be in the flesh, but here's what I believe God has just shared with me." I went on to tell them about the new vision I had received. After laying out the numbers I simply said, "Here's how you're going to know this is from God and not me. If it's from God, it will happen right before your very eyes. If it's not from God, it will not happen." I know that is not how you usually present a vision, but that is how I felt God told me to share it.

The people in the congregation were actually excited. Maybe it was because I hadn't really asked them to get involved in any specific way, but I was pleased with their response. Within a few weeks I developed a survey and sent it to everyone in the congregation. I asked them numerous questions about how they felt about the new vision. The vast majority, 90 percent of those who responded, wrote words of encouragement and excitement. Somewhere between 5 and 10 percent were negative in their responses. One person wrote, "Why do we need to grow anymore? I think we have enough people already." Others asked why we needed to focus on specific numbers. I don't know why it is, but often as pastors and leaders we forget the 90 percent who are positive and focus in on the small number of people who are negative. I was a little discouraged with the negative responses, and God seemed to say, "Just drop it for now."

For about six months I didn't say hardly anything about the new vision from the pulpit. Then one day my brother-in-law, who was a missionary in the Philippines, sent me an email. He said something like, "Jeff, I've heard about your vision to plant churches and we have a great planting movement over here. Would you be interested in joining our work by paying to build churches?" I wasn't thinking about planting churches overseas, but I mentioned it to the congregation, and without ever formally taking an offering, money started coming in to build churches in the Philippines. The organization there had a unique policy. They were planting in remote mountain villages and would only put up a building when they had developed 25 adult new converts. I have now lost track of exactly how many churches we and our other U.S. church plants have built in the Philippines, but it is somewhere between 15 and 20 churches. We also started paying the salaries of many of the pastors in these churches since they were in remote, extremely poor villages with very little potential for pastor's salaries and funds for other ministry expenses. Today, God is using these mountain churches to transform many, many lives.

After we started building the churches in the Philippines, it seemed like all other areas of the vision began to take off. By the time God called me to leave Parkway in 2011, we were averaging about 1,200 people in Sunday morning worship between Parkway and our church plants in America. We had about 50 full-time Christian workers in our school alone, plus dozens of others who had been called into full-time Christian service. And we had been empowered to be involved in the planting of more than 15 churches. Only God knows what impact the work of this vision will have on eternity. Truly, this has been and continues to be a supernatural work of the Holy Spirit.

As I am writing this book, Parkway is in the process of planting another church in the state of Virginia. This church is being planted by one of the young families that was saved in the early part of our ministry in Virginia.

Let me just briefly highlight each area where God has supernaturally worked in producing 1,000 new disciples, 100 full-time Christian workers, and 10 new church plants.

1000 New Disciples

I have learned through the years that when God gives a vision, He often works it out in ways beyond our ability to understand. We start out seeing it one way, and then as God unveils the vision, we go, "Oh, now I see." From 2000 to 2010 we saw hundreds of people come into our churches and either be saved or recommit their lives fully to Christ. It was never our desire to count decisions for Christ or even baptisms. We wanted to count people who had sold out to Christ. God raised up a new generation of disciples through our churches, school, and camps. Today, these disciples are ministering all over the U.S. and a number of other countries. Many of them have been called to other parts of God's vineyard, but they continue to serve Christ with a passion. God kept His word. I have mentioned a number of these disciples' individual stories throughout this book.

100 Full-Time Christian Workers

There are so many wonderful men and women I could highlight in this section. I hesitate to focus on one or two because I will leave out so many others, but I must bring God glory by sharing at least three stories with you.

Troy and Erica

When I moved to Parkway, I met a sharp young couple who were barely involved in the ministry of the church. Troy was the general manager of a local golf club as well as the golf pro at the club. He was often unable to attend church because of weekend tournaments where he worked. Erica had been a public school teacher, but was now a stay-at-home mom, which is a high and holy calling in and of itself. For some reason this couple stood out to me, and I visited them in their home. I sensed an eagerness in their hearts to be used more significantly by God. Troy soon came to a place of deeper surrender to Christ and things began to change.

One day he approached me and said that God had been talking to him. He went on to say that he believed God was asking him to leave the golfing business. Let me add here that every work we are involved in—whether in or outside the local church, whether in the pastorate, missions, business, sports, education, the arts, and so on—is a high and holy calling if God has led us to it. I do not elevate full-time Christian service above other callings because in reality every profession is full-time Christian service. However, having said that, God had specifically given us the vision of seeing 100 people called into full-time Christian ministry, and He was at work to make that happen. I will also add this. Even though every just work is noble, God does have a special call for certain people to give their lives 100 percent to the work of the ministry, and we need many more to make this commitment in our day. All of this said, I was a little surprised by Troy's declaration. I sure enjoyed the free golf and hot dogs he had been giving me! Nevertheless, I was thrilled that he was responding to God's call.

Troy quit the golfing business without another job in place. God provided a job for him that lasted about a year, and then God spoke clearly about his future ministry. I remember sitting in Troy and Erica's new house that had been built at cost by the company he went to work for after getting out of the golfing business. They had been earnestly praying about what God was calling them to do. As my wife and I were sitting in their living room, God spoke to me and said, "They are to help you start a Christian school." I looked at them and asked, "What would you think about helping us start a Christian school?" Instantaneously, they said "Yes!" That was in November 2001. By the fall of 2002, Parkway Christian Academy opened its doors with this young couple leading the way. For the last eleven years Erica and Troy have helped to build this school into one of the strongest Christian schools in our entire area. They have never been more challenged in their life, and yet they have never been more fulfilled. They know that choosing to accept God's offer into full-time Christian service has allowed them to impact more lives for Christ than they could ever possibly know.

Linda

Not long after moving to Parkway, I started interviewing to fill my secretary's position. There were several very qualified candidates, but I was drawn to a lady who had never worked in an office a day in her life. For some reason, I felt the Spirit's nudge to hire Linda. It didn't take me long to understand why God had led me to her. Linda loved the Lord, people, and the church. She quickly saw her job as her mission for Christ and would always go above and beyond to make sure my work was made effective. Over the eleven years we worked together, Linda became the hub of the church. People would often say, "Don't ask Pastor Jeff, ask Linda," and they were right to do so. At some point along the way, it became obvious that full-time Christian ministry was Linda's calling, not just her job. She eventually began to take mission trips and discovered that world missions would be her passion for the rest of her life. Today, Linda is the President of the Missions Department at Parkway and is influencing scores of men and women to give their life in service to Christ.

Recently she took a group of believers to Ukraine. On this trip she took her fifteen-year-old niece, Jill. Jill is an excellent student who has a passion for Christ and all things good. During her time in the Ukraine, God confirmed to Jill's heart her call to missions work, and she testified to this before the whole church. Linda's passion has now spread to the next generation in her family.

Once we start living the life of Radical Faith, God begins to repeatedly multiply our efforts and influence. Supernatural things begin to happen.

Jennifer

Jennifer came into our church in Roanoke having lived a very difficult life. From an early age she had struggled with clinical depression and had sought many different sources of help. Some were good and some were destructive. After surrendering her life fully to Christ, she began to volunteer in our church office. My assistant Linda, whom I mention in this section as well, began to love and disciple Jennifer. In spite of Jennifer's battle with depression, she began to blossom and grow. One day Linda asked her to try and design an insert for the weekly church bulletin and the rest, as they say, is history. We immediately discovered that Jennifer had a very natural gift in the field of graphic design. Her walk with Christ grew, and in spite of her constant concern with depression, her ability to design also grew. Today, Jennifer is the designer and editor of *The Renewanation Review* magazine and is responsible for the design and layout of the book you are reading. She still faces the challenge of depression, but God has given her a ministry that is changing people's lives. In her own words, this is how she describes what God has done for her.

> *"God enables me to do this ministry in spite of my depression. I've pleaded with God for healing, been prayed over countless times, and believe that He can fully heal me if He chooses to do so. I have told Him that if He wants to*

heal me, that's fine. If He doesn't, that's fine too. Whatever His will may be, I'm grateful either way.

There is a supernatural success that comes not only in the talents and ministry He has given me, but through the depression as well. There are many days when I say to Him, "God, I can't take this anymore! Please just let me be normal. I want to feel normal!" He says, "I am with you. I will not leave you. I will not forsake you." This battle of depression can sometimes be a minute by minute, second by second, dependence upon God, at times, just to live.

My job has grown far beyond me. Beyond my abilities. Beyond my capability to cope with the stress. I have to rely on God. Therein lies the supernatural success. It may not be what the world and some Christians see as successful, but it is success nonetheless."

10 New Church Plants

In the fall of 2002, God led us to start Parkway Christian Academy. Louise, a sweet grandmother, decided to volunteer her time at the school. She had several grandkids enrolled, and she was a great blessing.

One day as Louise was working in a classroom with a group of kids, she suddenly passed out and fell to the floor. When she fell, she hit her head and had to be taken to the hospital. Louise did not attend our church, but I felt the need to go to the hospital to check on her. She ended up being okay, so we had a few minutes to talk that day. During our conversation she said to me, "When my pastor retires, I plan on attending your church." I happened to know that her pastor was elderly and that her church was struggling. Her church was located near a lake about thirty minutes from the church I was pastoring. At our church, we had sensed that God might want us to plant a new church at the lake someday. I replied, "If your pastor ever retires, we might be interested in starting a new church out of the building you are worshiping in." She thought that was a nice idea, but we never talked about it again.

Three years later, on an icy Sunday morning in January, we decided to hold a service in spite of the fact that about every other church had canceled their services. I wasn't trying to be a hero, but I had a speaker from out of state and I wanted our people to hear him. As I was greeting the few brave souls who showed up that day, in walked Louise's pastor, "Bro. Clayton." He was there because his service was canceled. I asked him how he was doing, and he said, "Not too good." He then quickly added, "I'd like to talk to you about what you all talked about." I was scratching my head for a second trying to figure out what he meant. It then hit me that he was referring to the conversation Louise and I had three years ago. I asked him if he would like to come by and talk to me later in the week, and he said he would.

Bro. Clayton walked into my office on Thursday of the following week and said, "I'd like to give you the church building I've been using for the last forty-five years." He went on to say, "It's time for me to retire, and Louise said that you would like to start a new church using our building." I was stunned. I quickly told him what this would look like. I told him that we would close the current church, completely remodel the building, place all new people in leadership, rename the church, and start all over. He agreed with everything I said.

As he left I quickly began to call some of our leaders. Several people who had known strong-willed Bro. Clayton for many years said, "It will never happen."

Well, it did happen! We probably sent the largest crowd in the history of the church to celebrate his final service. We honored Bro. Clayton in every way we could as he handed the reins over to our organization.

The day before Bro. Clayton informed me that he was going to give us this church building, my brother Troy had received a word from the Lord that his pastorate at his church in Tennessee was complete. I called him as soon as I found out that we were going to have a facility at the lake and asked him to pray about being the lead pastor for this new church plant. I had tried to get Troy to join our team for years, but God had not allowed it. This phone call was different. I knew Troy was on his way.

We brought Troy's family and another pastor's family on staff for six months at Parkway. I encouraged every person in our church to pray about leaving and helping to plant the new church at the lake. On February 6, 2006, we commissioned seventy-six people to go and plant EastLake Community Church. This was a thrilling day as the vision God had given us was being fulfilled right before our eyes.

This was a thrilling day as the vision God had given us was being fulfilled right before our eyes.

As of the writing of this book, EastLake now averages 400 in Sunday morning attendance. They have led scores of people to

Christ and are making new disciples every week. One of their newest disciples is the recent Inspector General for the U.S. military in Afghanistan. At about 50 years old, this colonel has just retired and is leading the men's ministry at ELCC. His story of transformation is amazing as are so many others in this church plant.

It took Radical Faith to invest cash, people, and their tithe into this new plant. However, God replaced all of these things with more than we ever had before. There were tough times when our faith was tested, but we never averaged less in attendance or finances in any of the years when we gave a large group of people away. When we do what God tells us to do, we experience the supernatural success only He can produce.

The Power of Radical Faith

I am aware that many of the stories I have shared in this book relate directly to church ministry or people being called into ministry. I do not apologize for this; full-time Christian ministry is the arena in which God has called me to live and work, so I know it best. However, God is just as active in the lives of those Christians who do not spend every waking moment working around a church. One such example is Tony Feazell, a Christian businessman in construction.

Tony was saved through the Parkway church ministry in the 1960s. Through the 70s and 80s, the church struggled to grow, but Tony stood strong through every season of Parkway's history. There were many times when it looked like the church was going to die, but Tony never gave up. He built scores of homes throughout southwest Virginia and used the proceeds to fund the church's ministry. On many occasions it was his money that kept the doors open. Tony refused to give up even when the church dropped to only 40 to 50 in attendance. He kept praying and believing until God brought a new day.

In 1992, God brought Pastor Steve Parker to Parkway, and he and Tony led a charge to build a new church. Tony basically shut his construction business down for a year while he built the new church with no labor charges to the church. Scores of people were saved, and the church grew to 200 in attendance as a result of this new facility.

Over the last decade Parkway grew to over 650 in attendance and has now spawned numbers of new churches in Virginia alone. Over and over again Tony's financial support has made a huge difference. He gave the first $10,000 to start Parkway Christian Academy, the first $100,000 to start Renewanation and is still today a pillar in the church. Every time a soul is saved at Parkway, Tony is thrilled. He lives the surrendered life. He is willing to sacrifice greatly in order to support God's work. His passion for Christ and people is huge, and he has witnessed firsthand the supernatural power of almighty God.

God will bring supernatural success to any believer in any sphere of life who will radically trust and obey Him. The church worldwide needs millions of Christians in business, medicine, law, government, technology, and every other field who will do what God asks them to do. Will you be one of them?

Chapter 31

Renewanation

When I reached the stage of material success in my last pastorate, God asked me to leave it all behind and embark on a mission to make Christian worldview education available to every child in America. I was in a hotel in Cincinnati when God began to give me the vision of Renewanation. I thought I was doing pretty well in the ministry. Our church was healthy and growing; we were planting new churches; people were getting saved and being called to sell out to Christ. Our school was rapidly becoming the largest Christian school in our area. Our world mission efforts were expanding every year. What more could I do? On that November day in 2007, God spoke to me and said, "You're not going to simply be involved in giving a few hundred students a Christian worldview education. You're going to lead a drive to make it available to the masses." In the months and years that have followed this word from the Lord, I have been called to surrender my all once again.

Here at Renewanation we are already seeing many supernatural acts of God, but we are far from the place where we have some great story to tell. However, I am quite confident that within a few years we will have that story. It will not be a story of my success or anyone else's. This mission God has given us is so big that only He could ever make it a reality, and He will get the glory for it.

> This *mission* God has given us is so big that only He could ever make it a reality, and He will get the glory for it.

For now, we march forward without complete victory yet in hand. We face a daunting task as we enlighten people to the need for our children to receive a Christian worldview education. Some days it seems like everyone we talk to understands the task. On other days it seems like no one does. That's okay. It is our responsibility to be obedient to the call God has placed in our hearts. It is His responsibility to make His vision become a reality. Some might say to us, "That's a cop out." It could be if we were looking for an excuse not to give our very best, but we are not. We have sold our souls to Jesus, and we are daily paying the price of obedience to Him. We are not sufficient for the task, but He is. Consequently, someday I believe we will have an amazing story to tell of God's supernatural work to save the hearts, minds, and souls of millions of children.

Let me ask you. Are you experiencing the joy of living a life of Radical Faith? Do you know what it feels like to place your life completely in God's hands and leave the details up to Him? I hope so. The life of Radical Faith is the most fulfilling life you could ever live. But if you do not yet know this life and you want to, in the closing pages I give you the steps you must take in order to live this incredible life.

Join with me.

Better still, join with Jesus.

Give Him all you are and have.

Listen to Him.

Obey Him.

The life of Radical Faith is the most *fulfilling* life you could ever live.

Then watch Him accomplish great deeds in and through you.

Your life here and hereafter will never be the same.

Steps to a Life of Radical Faith

You must know for sure you have been saved.

Questions to ask:

Has there ever been a time when I truly experienced godly sorrow over my sin? Psalm 51

Have I repented of my sin (willful wrongdoing) and forsaken it? Mark 1:15; Acts 3:19

Have I fully trusted in Christ alone to save me? John 3:15-16; Acts 4:12

Have I experienced a changed life? 2 Corinthians 5:17; Ephesians 2:1-10

Do I have a strong desire to know and serve the Lord? Psalm 42:1

Does it grieve my heart when I stumble and fall into sin? Luke 24:54-62

Is my conscience tender? Genesis 39:9-10

You must, with God's help, be emptied of self and be filled with the fullness of Christ (the Holy Spirit).

Matthew 26:39; Acts 2:1-4; 15:8-9; Romans 6:1-22; 8:1-4; 12:1; Galatians 5:16-25; Ephesians 3:14-21; 5:18

Questions to ask:

Is there anything I am not willing to say or do for Christ?

Would I go anywhere He asks me to go, even if it meant I had to leave all that is known, convenient, and comfortable?

Do I love Christ more than my family, job, money, material things, recognition, position, reputation, or anything else?

Am I willing to look bad in other people's eyes if that's what following Christ requires?

Am I willing to look good in other people's eyes and still remain fully submitted to Christ?

Is the reigning desire of my heart one that wants to please God above all other desires?

Is my heart's cry the same as Paul's in Galatians 2:20? *"I have been crucified with Christ; it is no longer I who live, but Christ now lives in me."*

You must be walking in all the light God has given you.

1 John 1:7

Questions to ask:

Is there any area of disobedience in my life?

Am I presently overriding any leadings of the Holy Spirit?

Have I walked away from any truth that God has shared with me in the past?

In order for my heart and conscience to be clear before God, I need to seek His forgiveness for _____, right now.

You must live in His Word.

Romans 10:17; 1 Peter 1:22-2:3

Questions to ask:

Do I consistently read the Bible?

Do I listen to Scripture being read?

Do I study the Bible in some form on a regular basis?

Have I learned to study the Bible inductively? If not, a good place to start is: *The Joy of Discovery,* by Oletta Wald, or *Living by the Book,* by Howard and William Hendricks.

You must develop a habit of communing with God.

Questions to ask:

Do I set time aside just to pray?

Do I listen to God during my prayer time?

Is prayer one of my first responses when challenges arise?

Do I remain faithful in prayer until I receive a definite answer from God?

Am I often drawn to pray because I have no other options? This will be the case for those living the life of Radical Faith.

Do I pray with others in a small group?

Do I read good articles and books on the subject of prayer?

You must absorb sound biblical preaching and teaching.

Romans 10:17; Ephesians 4:11-12; 1 Timothy 4:6, 13; 2 Timothy 3:14-17

Questions to ask:

Do I attend a church where the preaching and teaching are biblical?

Does my preacher actually explain the Bible, or does he just use it as a jumping off point to speak on some topic that may have no real relevance to the biblical text?

Do I listen to good, biblical preachers and teachers outside of my local church?

Do I attend good Bible studies where the Word is mined for its riches?

You must live in fellowship with other Christians who strive to live the life of Radical Faith.

Questions to ask:

Do I have several Christian friends who are willing to obey God, no matter the costs?

Have I made myself accountable to Christians who practice the life of Radical Faith?

Do I mingle with missionaries and other Christians who are living the sold out life?

How much time do I spend with shallow, half-hearted Christians? Too much time with them will drain your passion for being sold out.

You must seek to stay fully surrendered at all times.

Matthew 22:37-38; Romans 6:12-13, 16, 19; 12:1-2; Hebrews 13:15-16

Questions to ask:

Am I willing to continue walking by faith even after I have fought and won major battles?

Do I believe I have a right to coast after living by Radical Faith for an extended period of time?

Am I accepting fleshly victories instead of trusting God for supernatural success once I have obtained the blessings by which I can manufacture success in the world's eyes?

Am I willing to continue doing what Christ has asked of me even if I do not see the results I hope for?

Prayers for Living by Radical Faith

For the Non-Christian:

Dear Jesus,

Thank you for making a personal relationship with you possible. I confess my sin and ask you to forgive me and come into my life. I believe you are my hope for salvation from sin and its punishment. I want to live the life of Radical Faith. I want to make a great difference for you and others in this life. Please forgive me for wasting so much time and help me to make up for lost time. I surrender my life fully to you as best I understand. Please take me and teach me what it means to follow you with all my heart and life. Thank you for loving me and accepting me into your family. Give me the strength to obey you no matter the cost from this day forward. Help me to always know that your way is the best way and that your way is the only way to live a life that experiences supernatural success. Thank you, Jesus, for hearing my prayer.

For the Christian:

Dear Jesus,

Thank you for loving me enough to save me from sin's power and punishment. Please forgive me for living a life in the flesh, and empower me to live a life under the full control of the Holy Spirit. I acknowledge that I have been afraid to trust you 100 percent. I acknowledge that I have wasted numerous opportunities and far too much time throughout my walk with you. I have often been more concerned with my personal comfort than I have been with lost people and the fulfillment of your mission on earth. Please teach me to live a life of Radical Faith. Please help me to know what that looks like for me, individually. Help me set the example for my family, friends, and fellow members of the Body of Christ. Please forgive me for my negative influence on those who thought my Christian life was the norm and have followed in my fleshly footsteps. Lord, I want to leave a spiritual legacy. I want you to look at my life and say, "Yes, that's what I'm talking about." I am so frail and know so little, but I submit my life to you, and with your help I will follow you wherever you lead. Fill me with your Holy Spirit and through this infilling, cleanse me and empower me to be the Christian you want me to be. Thank you for hearing and answering my prayer.

Our Vision

To offer millions of secularized children a Christian worldview.

renewanation

OFFERING EVERY CHILD A CHRISTIAN WORLD VIEW

Our Mission

PROMOTING the cause of K-12 Christian worldview education.

SUPPORTING Christian schools, Christian homeschools and ministries reaching public school students with Christian worldview training.

EXPANDING the number of children receiving Christian worldview training by being a catalyst to start many new schools, homeschools and ministries reaching public school students.

Find out more at renewanation.org

540-966-0648 • 1-855-TO-RENEW • P.O. Box 12366 Roanoke, VA 24025